A Banquet Without Wine:

A Quarter-Century of Liverpool FC in the Premier League Era

Anthony Stanley

Edited by Chris Rowland and Daniel Rhodes
Foreword by Paul Tomkins

A Tomkins Times' Book

www.tomkinstimes.com

For Catherine, Luke and Danny. My Premier League team.

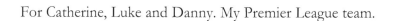

'To most Liverpool supporters, it wouldn't matter if eleven martians bring the championship back to Anfield, as long as it comes.' - Gérard Houllier.

'If you are first, you are first. If you are second ... you are nothing.' - Bill Shankly.

CONTENTS

ACKNOWLEDGMENTS

I would first like to thank Paul Tomkins who has been a constant source of inspiration over the last decade. The Tomkins Times, which has become far more important than just another Liverpool Football Club website, initially gave me a platform to scribble and to have my musings read by so many people whose views I respect.

To the editors, Chris Rowland and Daniel Rhodes, who combine an eagle's editorial eye with huge passion and knowledge for our football club, thanks for your encouragement and patience.

During the writing of this book, I have used many sources for research, in particular the work of John Williams and Simon Hughes has been invaluable, as has the marvelous Liverpool website LFCHistory.net.

To my wife Catherine, who has steadfastly endured my obsession for Liverpool, we will never walk alone.

Finally, I'd like to thank my parents. My mam, Paula, who fostered a love for the written word and dad, Tony, who has always believed.

FOREWORD

For Liverpool Football Club, the formation of the Premier League could not have come at a worse time. The perch that Alex Ferguson was so eager to knock the Reds from was, in fact, already broken; the club long-since fallen from it. Coming within just a few years of what I once called the club's "twin H-bombs" – Heysel and Hillsborough – the creation of the new league in 1992 coincided with the Reds being at their lowest ebb for decades.

And yet the past quarter of a century has not been without incident for the club – and, indeed, not without trophies too; all of which Anthony Stanley describes here with great skill. While football clearly didn't begin in 1992, despite what some people seem to think, it did mark the starting point of possibly the third major phase of the Reds' existence; after the 'early years', and the 'halcyon years' (1959-1990). While that simplifies several decades of pre-war football to some degree, the club's widespread fame stems from the point Bill Shankly took charge. And therefore, there is the pre-Shankly era, the bootroom era, and the post-bootroom era. It just happens to be that this almighty comedown coincided with the rebranding of English football.

By the summer of 1991, having been banned from European competition for six years, and with Kenny Dalglish having quit six months earlier under the clear strain of managing the club through the most traumatic time in its history, the new manager – Graeme Souness – inherited a difficult situation, and promptly made things worse.

By the time 1992/93 came around – the dawn of this shiny new era – the Reds had fallen to 6th in the table. With timing as perfect as Liverpool's was awful, Ferguson put United on their perch in the inaugural Premier League season – but only after Arsenal and Leeds United had won the league in that short period when Liverpool became also-rans. The new money rolling into the game went straight to Old Trafford, much of it bypassing Anfield – although the Reds were still major players in the transfer market; at least, for around five more years. By the end of the '90s

Liverpool had fallen a long way behind United, in terms of talent and also finances, and within a few more years came the new money of Roman Abramovich's Chelsea, and after that, Sheikh Mansour's billions at Manchester City, to further relegate the Reds down the pecking order. While the sport has always evolved, the past two-and-a-half decades has seen a sea change in English football. It became international, in almost every conceivable way.

My own story – and the story of the website on which this tome was first serialised – I first took myself to Anfield in 1990 as a midlands-based student in possession of an old second-hand car, and became a season ticket holder a few years later, once I'd graduated. For the best part of a decade I was a regular at home games (and at about half of the away matches), seeing the Reds' rises – and falls – under Roy Evans and then Gérard Houllier, before chronic illness put an end to my frequent attendances. Illness also cost me my career as a London-based designer, so I began writing about football as a hobby. At this very time, Houllier's Reds landed an historic cup treble. Suffice it to say it was one of those great seasons that would, alas, prove a mere outlier for the club in the era; peaks in the rollercoaster ride that often seemed to drag us down screaming (and puking) rather than pulling us up in ecstasy.

After Houllier came Rafa Benítez, a man whom I'd get to know personally during the latter part of his tenure, as a result of my weekly column for the official Liverpool FC website. As with Evans and Houllier, there were some really exciting times, and some frustrating times – but overall, it's clear that these were the best of the 25 years.

Liverpool reached two Champions League finals, winning one, and although the Premier League title remained elusive, the Reds' best points total in the revamped league came in 2008/09, when 86 was not enough against Man United's 90. The five years between 2004 and 2009 saw Liverpool as a hugely competitive force, ranked no.1 in Europe, before it all fell apart, with the help of the new, disruptive American owners, George Gillett and Tom Hicks. Thus began the great period of instability, on and off the field, although at the time of writing things appear to be getting back on track. Indeed, as of the summer of 2017, Liverpool are in far better shape than back in 1992 – finishing 4th in contrast to 6th, and with a world-class manager and a squad rich in potential. Unlike then, there are no key players who are ageing and melting. Liverpool could spend more money back then, relatively speaking (they were, along with Man United, the richest club), but history would prove how badly it was invested. And once spent – on players whose values withered away – there were virtually no resale values to reinvest (very expensive players like Paul Stewart and Nigel Clough left for nothing), and there was no Champions League money to help rebuild the side. If you buy the wrong players, and then cannot sell them, it's hard to progress as a club.

Still, for many clubs, the trophies won by the Reds in the past 25 years would represent some type of utopia (had that particular word not been infinitely sullied by Roy Hodgson's use of it to describe a draw at Goodison Park – that *he didn't even manage to achieve*). But between 1964 and 1990, Liverpool were no ordinary club. The yardstick was cruel when it came to measuring up.

My spending time with Benítez in October 2009 came just weeks after I'd launched *The Tomkins Times* website; originally designed to be my blog, but which developed into a much bigger entity. A year later, I was invited to have lunch with John W Henry, whose attempts to contact me via Facebook were ignored on the basis that I assumed it was a hoax. For a while I had a connection to the powers-that-be, and hopefully I can still speak with some authority on the club. What I will always look to do is give a platform to good writers (who also partake in interesting discussions), and Anthony certainly fits the bill.

Anthony first subscribed to the site in 2010, but only began posting comments in 2014. Within a few days we'd decided to turn one of his comments into an article, and since then he has written regularly for TTT. And now, just a few years later, here is *A Banquet Without Wine*.

The series of articles he wrote covering the Premier League era was crying out to be turned into a book, and so we asked him to flesh it out a little, and we now present it to you in this form. We sincerely hope you enjoy his account of a time when Liverpool won everything… except the one thing fans have increasingly wanted; but where – a few games here and there apart – there was rarely a dull moment.

Paul Tomkins, July 2017

CHAPTER 1 - TRADING PLACES

Looking back from our current vantage point, the world in 1992 – both footballing and in a larger sense – was at once familiar and strange. The toppling of the Berlin Wall had symbolically ushered in the end of Communism only a couple of years previously. A coalition of Western and Arab countries, under the virtual hegemony of the United States, had launched Operation Desert Storm the previous year, forcing Saddam Hussein's Iraq out of Kuwait. Nelson Mandela had recently been released from prison as the apartheid regime in South Africa was finally toppled. Bosnia–Herzegovina declared full independence and the Balkan Wars started in Eastern Europe, a harrowing conflict that would result in mass genocide and, eventually, UN intervention.

In the UK, the divisive reign of Margaret Thatcher had ended two years previously after mass demonstrations against the introduction of the hated Poll Tax, but political and social turmoil continued to rage, culminating in a three-day riot in Bristol a month before the inaugural Premier League season kicked off.

In the footballing arena too, it was a period of massive and rapid change. The Taylor Report, published in the aftermath of the horrific and tragic loss of life that was Hillsborough in April 1989, had recommended that all major stadia be converted to an all-seater model. Following this, in 1990, the Football League stipulated that all football grounds from the top two tiers of English football be all-seater by August 1994.

1990 was also, of course, the year when a nation fell in love with football again, and it's debatable whether the soon-to-be-seen garish razzmatazz of Sky Sports and its digital pay-per-view model would be the success it was if the English national team hadn't performed as they did and captured the hearts of the country. In particular, Paul Gascoigne, a genius of a footballer on his day but a vulnerable soul who struck a collective national chord of empathy, was possibly responsible more than anyone for the love affair that was about to begin between the sport and England. On a balmy night in Turin, his tears following a yellow card, which would mean he would miss the World Cup Final if the Three Lions beat Germany, entered a nation's consciousness. As Gary Lineker – another hero who encapsulated all that appeared to be good about the domestic game – gestured to Bobby Robson, an icon was born and with it a newfound positivity and optimism in football. Even as Chris Waddle skied his penalty and Robson – suddenly a beloved avuncular figure – looked on with exquisitely forlorn resignation etched on his face, the Thatcherite and grossly unfair portrayal of football fans as yobs and hooligans was firmly entering its death throes. Suddenly, it was cool to like football again.

If the formation of the Premier League was driven by the 'bigger' clubs wishing to procure greater financial rewards, the brassy Sky Sports was the fuel that ensured that the journey went further than anyone could have imagined. Satellite television guaranteed that the elite levels of the English game could be globalised; almost overnight, an insular and borderline myopic domestic game became a worldwide phenomenon, helped by the rapid strides in marketing and communication made possible by Sky and the corporation's vast reservoirs of cash.

Unfortunately for Liverpool, the birth of the Premier League and its Faustian deal with Sky came at the worst possible time; just when an embracing of modernity and all of its unique challenges was required, the club found itself ill-equipped to deal with this brave new world. The twin calamities of Heysel and Hillsborough had hit Liverpool very, very hard and essentially added to the decades-old philosophy of avoiding rather than embracing change.

Heysel and the subsequent banning of English clubs in Europe (with the Reds receiving an additional year to the domestic-wide five year ban), meant that a massive advantage on the field was now gone. Where previously the club's coaches had been exposed to differing playing styles and unique challenges abroad, the years following the disaster in Belgium – while full of success – nevertheless had more scope for stagnation. All of a sudden, for the first time since the 1964/65 season and the ensuing twenty one consecutive seasons of European football, the Reds didn't have the critical benefit of testing themselves against the best the continent could offer (this in an era where only one side qualified for UEFA's flagship competition). For example, after Johan Cruyff's developing Ajax side thrashed Liverpool in the Sixties, Bill Shankly had been alerted to the need for, as John Williams put it, 'far more flexibility and movement on the field, from defenders as well as forwards.' With the club reeling from the awful death toll in Brussels, with condemnation flying from every source and political manifestos being conjured on the quandary of a rampant culture of hooliganism, Liverpool's aura of invincibility was starting to fade.

But this blow was not a terminal one to the Reds' astonishing period of success and Kenny Dalglish, in the aftermath of Heysel, still created a prodigiously outstanding side, built around the formidable gifts of John

Barnes and Peter Beardsley and supplemented by the prolific John Aldridge. But as the Crazy Gang of Wimbledon prevented Liverpool from acquiring a second Double in two years, there were worrying signs abroad; two traditional powerhouses, Manchester United and Arsenal, were starting to get their act together following years in the wilderness. Liverpool would not have it all their own way for very much longer. Furthermore, there was another heartrending and tragic nail in the coffin of the Reds' domination of English football to come. The events of April 15th 1989 and the legacy of that awful day ensured that, to paraphrase Alex Ferguson, Liverpool were teetering on their perch of supremacy.

The club had always stressed continuity and stability, but in the aftermath of Hillsborough this bordered on arch-conservatism; the baggage of the disaster could not be easily cast off. Kenny Dalglish, even then a living legend, had carried much of the burden of the awful aftermath as funerals mounted up and he became the public face of a club in mourning. The Scot had wanted to resign in the summer of 1990 but had been persuaded to stay on by the board. However, it rapidly became apparent he was under huge strain, cutting an increasingly haggard and troubled figure. Some of his last signings for the club symbolised that he had, by his own admission, taken his eye off the ball and lost that crucial characteristic of assertiveness.

Towards the end of his reign, his signings were curious to say the least; Jimmy Carter, David Speedie and Nicky Tanner could hardly be placed in the same bracket as the brilliant triumvirate of Barnes, Ray Houghton and Beardsley. Moreover, the worn-down and gaunt Dalglish had failed to act with an obviously ageing side; amidst all the Hillsborough aftermath, Paisley's old adage that players' legs should grow old on another team's pitch had understandably been forgotten. Dalglish's resignation may have come as a shock to the footballing world, but hindsight shows us that it should have been anything but.

In his masterful biography of Liverpool, *Red Men*, John Williams again makes the succinct point that:

'Crucially, all this emotional upheaval, disruption and uncertainty for Liverpool Football Club also happened at a critical moment in the development of the English game. Liverpool had fallen behind the rest of English football in the 1920s because of tactical inadequacy and in the 1950s because of board-room penny pinching. Now it would fall behind again.'

There would be no bouncing back this time. As Graeme Souness prepared for his second full season as Liverpool manager and the Premier League got ready for its assault on the national mindset, the Reds were suddenly in their most perilous position in decades. Just as the commercial and marketing aspect of the game was rapidly coalescing into something approaching its current incarnation – a world of vast, dizzying sums of money, as foreign to Shankly's egalitarian vision as one could reasonably expect – the Reds were in the worst conceivable shape to cope. To put it simply, the coming (and timing) of Sky and the Premier League was catastrophic for a reeling Liverpool Football Club.

The first ever game in the Premier League saw two of the big hitters of the late Seventies face off against each other as Liverpool travelled to Nottingham Forest's City Ground. Against a backdrop of mass stadium renovation as Forest prepared to comply with the Football League's seating stipulation, a Teddy Sheringham rocket gave Brian Clough's charges victory. Souness, already under pressure following a sixth place finish the previous year and the crassness of him selling a story of his heart operation to the reviled Sun newspaper on the anniversary of Hillsborough, could probably see the looming thunderhead.

The Scot, more than any other factor, carries the blame of most fans for the travails of Liverpool in the early nineties and, though he made massive mistakes, he took on the manager's job when the running of the side was arguably as challenging as at any time in the club's history. The perceived wisdom is that Souness, as well as alienating some of the senior players in the side, sold first teamers too soon and replaced them poorly. While this may be true, the Scot did seek to innovate and recognised that the club was in danger of falling behind the rest of football's modernisation. Where he ultimately failed however, was in the brashness of his personality and his poor recruitment. The signings in 1992 testify to this; Paul Stewart and Torben Piechnik had more than a few eyebrows raised in bewilderment while Ray Houghton and Dean Saunders were offloaded to Aston Villa and would promptly take part in a title challenge under Ron Atkinson.

Liverpool had been completely outplayed by Forest (who would end the season relegated) and the 1-0 scoreline flattered the Reds. Although the Anfield club were seen by the media as one of the early season favourites to win the Premier League, by October this was already a pipedream, in an early indication of what was to come in future seasons. On Halloween, Liverpool served up a horror show in a 2-0 defeat away to Tottenham Hotspur, a result that saw the Reds languishing in fourteenth place after their sixth loss. Liverpool were floundering and Souness was swimming against a tide of widespread condemnation from Kopites and the Scot's former teammates. Nor could the Liverpool manager find solace in the media as *The Guardian* referred to a side who had won the title just two years previously as 'faded aristocrats.'

But few could argue with this assertion a week before Christmas when a beleaguered Souness took his charges to Coventry City, only to meekly retreat following an abject 5-1 thumping, Liverpool's heaviest league defeat since 1977. This, following a comically inept exit in the European Cup Winners' Cup to Spartak Moscow (6-2 on aggregate to the Russians), meant that the writing was well and truly on the wall for Souness.

The Reds did rally in the second half of the season and this probably delayed the hangman's noose that the Scot must have felt gripping his neck for much of his tenure. However, Liverpool still finished sixth and, horrifyingly to Kopites, also found themselves twenty five points behind the first champions of the Premier League, Manchester United.

Souness was backed in the transfer market before the 1993/94 season with the big money arrivals of Nigel Clough and Neil Ruddock joining Julian Dicks in the Liverpool ranks. The season started promisingly, with three wins in a row and ten goals scored. But the barely concealed cracks soon reappeared when the Reds meekly capitulated to Spurs at Anfield, going down 2-1. A familiar, depressing pattern was about to play itself out and when Liverpool were hammered 3-0 by an Andy Cole-inspired Newcastle United in late November, they were already seventeen points behind United, the early pace setters in the league.

At least Kopites had been given something to cheer about when a young, fearless Scouser called Robbie Fowler helped himself to an astounding five goals in a League Cup tie against Fulham. The little scally, reared in Toxteth and adored by the Kop from day one, was catapulted into the league first team, but even his embryonic goalscoring genius could not halt what was now a full-blown decline. A memorable 3-3 draw against the old rivals from Manchester was another brief respite but it spoke wretched volumes that coming back from 3-0 down to secure a point against the champions provoked such delirious celebration. In a very short period of time, Liverpool had plummeted to hitherto unforeseen and unimagined depths, and when Bristol City defeated the Reds 1-0 in an FA Cup Third Round replay at Anfield on a freezing January night, Souness' time was up. After thirty-three months and having presided over £30 million worth of transfers in that time, the Scot resigned. A club statement was released in which Souness claimed:

'I took this job believing that I could return the club to its former glory but this proved to be more difficult than I anticipated. The fans have been very patient but I feel that their patience is now running out. Liverpool Football Club has, and always will have, a very special place in my heart and I can only wish the club well and every success in the future. I wish to thank the chairman, the board and everyone else associated with the club for their help and support which they have given me during my term as manager.'

As Liverpool chairman John Moores (a close personal friend of the Scot) stated, there had been mitigating circumstances in Souness' failure such as the death of his father, the trauma of heart surgery and an ever-lengthening injury list. But, as has been highlighted, the truth of the matter was that Souness displayed poor man-management and an even poorer eye for a player; two absolutely vital areas of any top level manager. However, on the credit side, he blooded two future stars in Steve McManaman and

Fowler and sought valiantly to modernise the club. And it should not be forgotten that the job of Liverpool manager was at that particular juncture in the Nineties, as it is now, one of the hardest in football.

As football continued to swiftly evolve in this country and abroad, the Liverpool board again looked to resurrect the past and, with the appointment of the loyal and likeable Roy Evans, sought to revive the Boot Room culture that had served the club so well in the past. Bootle-born Evans had been at the club in some capacity for thirty years and he himself always thought he was being groomed for the top job eventually. Though he spoke reassuringly to Kopites about bringing back the traditions of the Liverpool Way and the Boot Room, there was a troubling spectre of the club steadfastly refusing to follow the lead of the rest of a rapidly and profoundly changing English footballing landscape.

However, there was undoubted optimism in the appointment; hindsight may tell us that the club was still entrenched a little too firmly in the *ancien regime* of its traditions in the face of the shifting nature of English football but, lest we forget, Evans actually did a good job. Unfortunately, the terrain had altered to such a degree that it could be argued that the appointment smacked a little too uncomfortably of anachronism.

If Evans was in any doubt about the size of the job he had inherited, this was laid to rest when Liverpool found themselves 4-0 down against Southampton inside forty nine minutes in the Bootle native's second game in charge. Results fluctuated and inconsistency abounded for the rest of the campaign, and by the time Manchester United, on their way to a first league and cup Double themselves, defeated the Reds 1-0, Liverpool were twenty three points behind their historical rivals (it should be noted that the attendance that day in Old Trafford was 44,751 – the days of United becoming a cash-laden behemoth were still in the future and the Reds could still compete – if not on the field – then at least financially with their near neighbours). Liverpool eventually finished eighth in the table with Blackburn Rovers, Sheffield Wednesday and Wimbledon all ahead of them in the final standings.

For Roy Evans, desperate to help his club rejoin the elites of the domestic game, the hard work was just about to start.

CHAPTER 2 – EVANS HELP US

As Roy Evans took his seat in the visitors' dugout at Selhurst Park on a bright, early autumn afternoon in 1994, perhaps he cast his mind back over the incredible path that had taken him to this moment. It had been a journey that had taken thirty years; from a player who just failed to make the grade at the highest level under Shankly to being groomed by the Liverpool hierarchy as a potential first team manager. Evans may well have blinked into the sun and swallowed tears of pride – he knew the enormity of the job and what success in his inaugural full season would mean to the passionate and frenzied Liverpool support.

The new Liverpool manager would later recount the daunting juxtaposition of where he now found himself to Simon Hughes in *Men in White Suits* (there we are, the suits have been mentioned in the second paragraph, at least indirectly):

'I'm not sure that being a fan of the team you manage is necessarily a good thing. The doubts start the first time you get beaten … you realise what it means to so many people … When you lose, you realise how it can spoil a person's day or week. It's your feelings multiplied by forty-five thousand people at Anfield and those watching on TV or listening on the radio… it wasn't nice if we'd lost, you felt like you'd let people down, there was a horrible feeling deep in your stomach.'

Evans may have clearly been a passionate fan, but there would, evidently, be no sentimentality. The dust had barely settled on the reconstruction of the Kop to an all-seater stadium, before he had flogged some of Liverpool's finest servants from the 1980s; Ronnie Whelan, Steve Nicol and Bruce Grobbelaar joined the pedestrian and overweight Julian Dicks, the ineffective Torben Piechnik and the undisciplined Don Hutchison towards the exit door. In came John Scales, Phil Babb and Mark Kennedy. The former two would form a formidable footballing back three with a rejuvenated Mark Wright in Evans' new 5-3-2 system. A reinvented John Barnes – shorn of his electric pace due to an Achilles injury – would pull the strings in midfield with Jamie Redknapp and the loping, ultra-talented Steve McManaman, who sometimes appeared lost under Souness but was about to fulfil his brilliant potential. The finishing icing on this creative cake was the goalscoring genius of the nineteen-year-old urchin, Robbie Fowler.

Things started well for Evans and his new look Reds. The pregnant, heavy and grey storm clouds that had hung over Anfield for the previous two years were not quite swept away but there was tangible sunshine present as the mood of the fans lifted. Kopites were fully behind the appointment of the new manager; a back-to-basics approach was viewed as badly needed following the damage that had been done by Evans' abrasive predecessor. Nor was the new boss – contrary to popular myth – allergic to modernity. Roy brought in Doug Livermore – then Spurs' joint caretaker-manager – as his assistant and also became the first Liverpool boss to appoint a full-time goalkeeping coach in Joe Corrigan. Later, physio Mark Leather was also brought in, joining Sammy Lee and Dr Mark Waller in a new look Boot Room. Evans may have been talking the back-to-basics line (which would become a hideous media cliché by September of 1994) but he wished to marry his own vision with that which he had, in a footballing sense, been brought up on. As the manager stated:

'It's always been my style to let everyone chip in with suggestions, just as I had been encouraged to do when I first joined the Boot Room.'

The 1994/95 season started with a bang and a deluge of goals. Only four years since winning the old First Division title – and well before the arrival of the game-changing Chelsea and Manchester City billions – Liverpool were seen as genuine title challengers, even if their chances were seen as much weaker than the new dominant force, a Manchester United that had finished a distressing thirty two points ahead of the Reds in the previous season. But Kopites, then as now, needed little prodding in order to dream and when Liverpool started the season with three straight wins and eleven goals scored, there was a sense that we could be reacquainted with our perch. Amongst these early victories, the 3-0 hammering of Arsenal at Anfield will live long in the memory of anyone who was present, with the astonishing Fowler helping himself to a hat-trick inside a delirious four minutes and thirty three seconds, a record that stood until 2015 when Sadio Mané improbably accomplished the feat in just under three minutes. The Kop – now ostensibly forced to sit – had a new hero and spent the game standing in adoration of a young man that was about to be christened 'God'.

To those who weren't around for the coming of Fowler, it's hard to describe just what it was that provoked such worship from Liverpool fans. Obviously his nerveless finishing and precocious ability was a big part of the draw, but there was so much more. Robbie was an icon, made for

Liverpool fans; a squattish lad who didn't appear like a natural athlete, who didn't have particularly good pace, who – and even more so when footballers weren't so removed from the fans – looked like one of us. Had this lad wandered on to the pitch from the stands? But then that left foot would swing and Anfield would erupt. Robbie scored goals from all over the pitch, a dizzying amount, and this is perhaps encapsulated by his historic hat-trick against Arsenal. Sometimes Robbie seemed bemused and self-deprecating (of the glut of goals against the Gunners he remarked: 'I didn't really know the goals came so quickly, I thought they were fifteen minutes apart') and though there were some indiscretions looming in his future, if anything, these merely added to his legend.

Evans was aware of what he had at his disposal in the Toxteth terrier. 'The lad Fowler is obviously an immense talent, frightening,' he beamed.

Then there was McManaman, who took Fowler under his wing. Sharp and university-bright, wiser in the ways of the world than his younger teammate and a player whose huge gifts have – to a degree – been airbrushed from the memory of many Liverpool supporters. But as Jamie Carragher – then coming through the ranks at Liverpool – wrote in his autobiography:

'His performances under Roy Evans deserve far more recognition than they're given now. People seem to forget he virtually single-handedly won two cups for Liverpool. The 1992 FA Cup win under Souness was McManaman's tournament in every round, and he inspired the sole cup success under Evans, the 1995 League Cup against Bolton.'

That, as the next few seasons progressed, the opposition mantra became increasingly 'stop McManaman, stop Liverpool' shows his contribution and talent.

It was a season of undoubted progress and encouragement. Old heads Barnes and Rush helped to guide the young guns who were making waves and Liverpool fans delighted in the rebirth of a proper pass and move game (even if this was sometimes overdone). In the league, the Reds would finish fourth, behind new champions Blackburn Rovers (who, memorably, secured their title in defeat at Anfield with a grinning Kenny Dalglish – their manager – waving to the adoration of both sets of supporters). Manchester United finished second and Nottingham Forest completed the top three. There was a clear sense amongst Liverpool supporters that further progress could be made in 1995/96 given the relative youth and talent in the squad.

The Coca-Cola Cup gave Evans his first (and only) trophy that season as Liverpool, overcoming Blackburn and Arsenal en route, marched to the final in April against Bolton Wanderers. A young Steve McManaman produced a mesmerising display that would have his name forever linked with a Wembley showpiece. The twenty three year old winger scored two solo goals of breathtaking quality to spell defeat for Bruce Rioch's spirited charges. It felt like the start of something and it seemed that the appointment of Evans and a reintroduction of old values had been an inspired one.

In many ways the following campaign, 1995/96, was the apogee of Evans' fluid 5-3-2 system and a season which many Liverpool fans still gaze back at fondly – even if there were disquieting rumours and developments starting to be spoken in hushed tones. Evans brought in Jason McAteer to play wingback following his sterling showing in the Coca-Cola Cup Final for Bolton. But it was another arrival – for a then British transfer record – that was a massive risk and one that ultimately failed. It's easy to look back with hindsight but essentially the signing of Stan Collymore from Nottingham Forest was, in many ways, the beginning of the end for this exciting side that Evans had forged and was tantamount to the Liverpool boss signing his own managerial death warrant.

Collymore, a complex individual and one in whom it is perhaps easy to be overly harsh, was nevertheless a caustic and corrosive influence on the Liverpool dressing room. He possessed massive ability and huge natural talent and on his day could be a world beater; the problem was that this 'day' became more and more infrequent as his career in red progressed and, for the vast majority of the bigger games, Collymore simply never showed up. But Evans thought that the Nottingham Forest forward could win the Reds the league and so sanctioned the £8.5 million deal. In fact, the former Liverpool manager must look back on this roll of the dice with particular regret – Evans claimed later that Collymore and Ronaldo (the real one) had comparable ability. The Brazilian was then at PSV Eindhoven and about to become a bona fide superstar and, of the two, Evans claimed:

'On the face of it, there wasn't much difference. They both had power, pace, skill and a great finishing ability. I'd considered Ronaldo … but it boiled down to Stan being English and knowing the demands of the country and the Premier League.'

While comparing Collymore to one of the greatest strikers of all time may seem unlikely, what really is of note here is Evans's comments pointing to a lingering insularity, weaned over success filled decades, that still dogged the club.

Indeed, Ronnie Rosenthal, signed by Dalglish a couple of seasons before Evans got the job, went further when dissecting the transfer philosophy of the club:

'Liverpool was still a very conservative club, which only really wanted to sign the best British players. But (by the mid-nineties) they had a lot of competition for these players. Leeds came, United were becoming stronger, Arsenal were there. Liverpool lost its domination of the league. For a long time, the club could get away with paying lower wages for players because of its history. Then – now, even – it wasn't there to fall back on.'

This, then, is the crux of the matter; post-Hillsborough conservatism is one thing, but the football club missed the boat again during Evans's tenure – stabilisation was welcome but perhaps something more radical was actually needed. While Liverpool were recruiting Collymore and McAteer, Arsenal managed to sign Dennis Bergkamp and Spurs had previously pulled off a coup in landing Jürgen Klinsmann. Even Chelsea – well before Russian money arrived – were going out and snaring Ruud Gullit and Gianfranco Zola. Nor could this be explained as a 'lights of London' development; little Middlesbrough swooped for the Brazilian Juninho at around the same time. It would take another couple of years before the club fully embraced this new face of modern domestic football by which time Arsenal – another giant who had been rooted in traditional conservatism – had appointed Arsène Wenger and secured the likes of Nicolas Anelka, Patrick Viera and Emmanuel Petit. The Londoners enjoyed a massive head start on Liverpool, one from which the Reds are (arguably) still striving to recover from.

But for all that, 95/96 was still a hugely enjoyable season, particularly when juxtaposed with what had gone before (even if it's tempting to speculate what a Juninho or Klinsmann may have added; never mind a Ronaldo). Liverpool played the best football in the country; a gorgeous passing style that was pleasing on the eye and could be devastating to the opposition (though there was often a lingering doubt about the Reds' ruthlessness). With Fowler (who would break the thirty goal barrier for the second season in a row) and McManaman dovetailing superbly, supported by Collymore (whose first season was actually a solid, if hardly prolific, one) and with Barnes and Redknapp pulling the strings and the overlapping Rob Jones and McAteer bombing on constantly, Liverpool were looking like a genuine force again. It ultimately ended in disappointment, but a third place finish (narrowly missing out on a Champions League spot which was then only awarded to the top two) and some memorable matches made the season a qualified success.

Two games, more than any others, probably sum up the joys, frustrations and lows of the season and could act as a microcosm for the campaign as a whole. The breathtaking 4-3 victory over Newcastle in April, which simultaneously was the final nail in the Geordies' title challenge while seeming to reignite the Reds' chances, was a glorious display of attacking football by two sides brimming with lethal intent. The game was just what Sky's still developing model had hoped for and it would become symbolic of the crazy, helter-skelter nature of the hugely entertaining Premier League, although it was all too easy for tabloids to seize on lazy and facile deductions. Though Newcastle United under Kevin Keegan did attack to the detriment of their defence throughout that year, Liverpool's defensive record was, contrary to the popular imagination, very good (only Arsenal conceded fewer goals that season in the entire league while the Reds also boasted the second best defensive record in Evans' first full season).

But there was a trend developing; decisive defensive mistakes were being made at key moments of massive games – this, rather than a consistently soft underbelly, was the common denominator that was beginning to manifest itself in Evans' Liverpool. This wasn't the Liverpool of Dalglish, Hansen, Souness and Nicol, hewn from hard Scottish granite who married ability and toughness. This was a young side that had to deal with the massive pressures that was the legacy of their predecessors plus more frequent diversions off the pitch.

However, it would be bordering on churlish to glean anything but positivity from that night at Anfield. A game that ebbed and flowed with breathless, relentless and daring attacking, like two boxers slugging it out in a ring, neither prepared to put their guard up, both aware that this could go either way. It was Liverpool who emerged victorious as Stan Collymore, after some wonderfully intricate passing from the veterans Barnes and Rush in a packed penalty area, lashed home the winner with seconds left. Cue scenes of delirium from the Anfield crowd and Keegan practically trying to sink into the advertising hoarding. Liverpool, with a few Premier League games left, were suddenly on the march again. At least they were until Coventry City defeated the Reds in the following game. Liverpool would finish third, eleven points behind Manchester United. The Reds had flirted intermittently with a title challenge without ever quite getting there but, nevertheless, progress had undoubtedly been made.

For far less positive reasons, the FA Cup Final was another defining moment of the season – and, arguably, of Evans' entire Liverpool managerial career. No fashion faux pas will be mentioned at this juncture (this will be touched on in the next chapter) but there was crushing disappointment and frustration when the Reds pitched up to do battle with Manchester United at Wembley. Kopites anticipated victory; Liverpool – and in particular Robbie Fowler – had the measure of United. Twice in the league the Reds had utterly outplayed their northern rivals; at Old Trafford, Robbie Fowler had scored two exquisite goals only for a returning Eric Cantona to equalise with a contentious penalty. At Anfield, however, the Reds had taken United apart with a free kick and cannily finished goal from that man Robbie. Moreover, the run to the final itself had been a thing of beauty as the Reds served up thrilling attacking football and scored nineteen goals on the way to Wembley. Fowler's brace – a sumptuous, dipping volley into the top corner and a diving header – in the semi-final dismantling of Aston Villa seemed to symbolise this swashbuckling verve. Surely it was destiny for this Liverpool side to win the FA Cup? Surely that consolation was ours, after United had again secured the league? Surely we'd prevent them from achieving another Double?

You know the rest. The final was the definition of a damp squib. Ferguson, determined not to be exposed by Liverpool's dynamic duo of Fowler and McManaman, played the pragmatic card (not for the last time against the Reds) and the two teams essentially cancelled each other out. Frustration reigned among both sets of supporters as the game entered its final moments. Then capricious fate struck. David James came for a routine David Beckham corner and, in what would become a depressingly familiar sight, flapped at the ball, sending it towards the lurking Cantona. The Frenchman volleyed it straight back towards goal, through what seemed like approximately seventy three bodies, and as it nestled in the net, Liverpool supporters knew, with grim resignation, that there was no way back.

Liverpool and Evans were left to reflect on what may have been; a season that had promised so much had delivered very little. The Reds had played some breathtaking football and there were tangible signs of progress. But there was a troubling spectre in the background, one that would become increasingly apparent and one in which the attire before the final only hinted at. Mere weeks after the FA Cup Final no-show, as a nation rocked to 'Football's Coming Home' and danced to the footballing beat of Terry Venables' England, a girl band released 'Wannabe' and became a tabloid writer's dream. The band was The Spice Girls and a hack journalist was about to strike gutter press gold with a moniker that would haunt Evans and his team throughout the next two seasons.

CHAPTER 3 - THE SPICE OF STRIFE

'Listen, you can call them Spice Boys or whatever you want, but when they played football matches, they wanted to win. The attitude was always good when it came to the game. Did we fulfil our promise? Probably not. On our day we were as good as anybody but our day didn't come quite often enough. The outside stuff – when players went home – it was irrelevant.'

— Roy Evans, speaking to Simon Hughes for Men in White Suits in 2014.

Except of course, the outside stuff was not irrelevant. It may have been if the team were winning but increasingly the host of extracurricular activities became the overriding narrative of Evans' side; the sideshow became the story, to the gleeful mirth of tabloids up and down the country.

The reality is painted not in black and white but, like all aspects of life, in nuanced shades of varying colours. Evans was not blameless but was also not the weak, spineless manager many portrayed him to be. The players – and predictably many deny the accusations – must take some of the blame, but theirs was a unique generation, straddling the drinking culture of the Seventies and Eighties with what was becoming an ultra-professional game consisting of finely tuned athletes. The billions pumped into football in the Nineties and the new-found universal adulation meant footballers suddenly found themselves cast as the new rock stars; the zeitgeist of the time was cool Britannia, Brit Pop and its ilk. The representatives of the big clubs were – for the first time in history – placed on a pedestal with the likes of Damon Albarn, Robbie Williams and Liam Gallagher. Lee Sharpe and Ryan Giggs were guilty of off the field excesses, for example, but they had an authoritarian manager whose success had enabled the use of an iron fist. As Paul Tomkins notes in Dynasty, Roy Evans was not 'especially weak – it was just that he wasn't strong enough consistently enough.'

Cracks and fissures had appeared in the Liverpool dressing room during Souness' turbulent regime; team spirit was so low that apparently only six first team players turned up for a celebratory jaunt to Tenerife following the FA Cup victory of 1992. Evans sought to heal the rifts by permitting more sociable behaviour and treating the players like adults, relying on the old guard like Barnes and Rush to pull in the more boisterous behaviour. It had, after all, worked for the club in all the decades that Roy had been at Liverpool; the more senior figures in the dressing room could always be counted on to curb any excess. But, like so much that happened in the Nineties, the timing was all wrong. Football was changing rapidly and Liverpool Football Club needed to embrace the modernity. But, from the very top, the club was again guilty of an anachronistic wallowing in the past. This laxness was bound to trickle down; that's not an excuse for the players and their misdemeanours but it has to be taken into consideration when analysing the time.

John Scales, signed by Evans from Wimbledon, made some interesting points in a recent interview in *The Telegraph* and essentially claimed that Liverpool were caught in a time warp. Having moved from the self-styled Crazy Gang, Scales was anticipating the epitome of professionalism, sophistication and good practice from his new club; the reality came as a grim surprise:

'Ronnie Moran's training had not changed since that time. The wooden target boards were still used and they were rotting away. There was no tactical or technical analysis. Diets did not come into any discussion. For away games, we'd turn up in jeans – just as all the players had done in the '70s. There were so many bad habits. Mentally, the team was underprepared at a time football clubs were figuring out, like the rest of the world, that mental health improves physical performance.'

Scales went on to highlight the fact that, not only was Melwood underdeveloped, but the only official merchandising was 'a small shop in the corner of the carpark.'

Compare this with Manchester United's rapidly growing corporate behemoth and it becomes rapidly apparent that David Moores must share some of the blame. As Scales argues:

'In any walk of life, if you give people an inch they'll walk a mile, especially young lads. Roy wasn't necessarily too nice. But maybe he was too lenient. Above Roy, the chairman David Moores could have been more forceful on a lot of issues. If a club does not have structure, then it's not going to function on the pitch in the long term. The whole approach at United was more professional from top to bottom.'

In short, the club was enveloped in a troubling, anachronistic miasma that was suffocating any chance of real success. Football was becoming a game of percentages; at the highest level, every resource that could improve a team's chances had to be taken without hesitation, every potential advantage had to be embraced. The Reds, despite possessing footballers of aesthetic brilliance during the decade, simply failed to adhere to this adage.

It was from this pool of relative stagnation that the media monster – the Spice Boys – arose, dripping with negative tales of excess.

Cultural changes were sweeping through the game in England and the players possessed all the cards. As Derek Dohren wrote in his biography of Roy Evans:

'modelling contracts, high-powered agents, advertising deals and pop-star girlfriends were now the norm for those lucky enough to be plying their trade with one of the top Premiership teams.'

This was not just the preserve of Liverpool players; by no means did they possess a monopoly here. David Ginola, for example, good looking and cavalier, a symbol of Keegan's Newcastle United, cringe-inducingly claimed that he was 'worth it' in an advert for a hair product. But Newcastle players didn't (and don't) sell tabloids in the way that Liverpool Football Club does. Always one of the favourites for the Premiership, it was the very potential for greatness inherent in Evans' side that ensured they would bear the brunt of any media backlash on apparently spoiled, pampered and unprofessional footballers. The talented Reds came to be seen as the epitome of the distressing culture that was sweeping through the domestic game; Jamie Redknapp, David James and Robbie Fowler (the latter of whom was rumoured to be dating Baby Spice at one stage) became the (slightly facile) faces of underachievement.

But none of this is to exempt the Liverpool players of blame. There is a direct correlation with on-field frustrations – and there were plenty – and lurid front page tabloid headlines. Despite there being more than a whiff of exaggeration about the whole 'Spice Boy' phenomenon, a phrase that was originally coined by the *Daily Mail* and seized on by paragons of apparent virtue everywhere, there are some facts that cannot be argued with. Rumours, counter-arguments and dubious claims by former players are one thing but there was serendipity about the developments within and without the Liverpool squad that didn't help those who protested that it was nonsense. Rob Jones – soon to be struck down by a career-ending injury – became close friends with Robbie Williams, just before the singer left the boy band Take That. As a result, Williams ended up getting invited onto the team bus for a trip to Aston Villa. The singer, now battling alcoholism, drug addiction and weight gain following his split from the band, also accompanied a group of players which included John Barnes on an end of season jaunt to Magaluf. Jamie Redknapp – seen by many as the epitome of the Spice Boys moniker, a player who underachieved due to off the pitch excess (not that this is the case) – started dating Louise Nurding, a singer in the girl band Eternal, in 1996. There were pictures all over the tabloids of Robbie Fowler out with Emma Bunton, also known as Baby Spice. Jason McAteer started dating lad's mag favourite Donna Air, and the less said about that advert the better. David James was frequently jetting off to the cat walks of Milan to model underwear. All of this contributed to a general sense that the Liverpool players' priorities were not what they should be. Of course, it didn't help that Fowler and Redknapp would later sustain debilitating injuries, curtailing their time on the pitch and adding to the overall impression. The latter told Simon Hughes:

'It progressed quicker than anyone could comprehend, when you consider players were having beers and fish and chips on the bus after games just a few years earlier.'

There may be more than a hint of 'methinks he doth protest too much' here from the former Reds' midfielder. Redknapp, along with Scales, Babb and McAteer, would frequently jet off to Heathrow from Manchester airport directly after a Saturday afternoon game. There, the quartet would drop their bags at the Halkin Hotel and head out to the likes of the Emporium, the Chinawhite and the Tea Rooms; the trendy preserve of the rich in Soho. Redknapp conceded that: 'if I had my chance again, I probably wouldn't have done it as much.'

But even as he says this, the former Liverpool midfielder consistently makes excuses for his lifestyle in the 90s:

'In some places, I'd see Ryan Giggs and the United boys. In fact Giggsy'd be out a lot more than me. I'd be tucked up in bed and Giggsy would be out. The difference is, nobody cares when you're winning. If you're just falling short, everybody wants to let you know about it.'

Yes, Jamie, but perhaps you're missing the point. Perhaps you may not have been 'just falling short' if you had, in fact, been 'tucked up in bed' more often. Though there may be some sympathy for Redknapp and his cohorts and the treatment they got from the media, the fact is that they were earning tens of thousands a week. Tucked up in bed was perhaps the least we, as supporters of the club, expected and deserved.

The suits – the awful, cream suits (procured by David James thanks to his Armani contacts) and hitman style shades which were worn by the jocular, jesting and joking players prior to the 1996 FA Cup Final, symbolise all of this. Redknapp claimed that no one would remember the attire if they had won and perhaps he was right, but there was a general lack of focus and discipline at the club that cannot be ignored. Unfortunately, there is just no getting away from that.

CHAPTER 4 - ROBBIE AND MICHAEL

'Robbie Fowler? He could have been the brother of any Liverpool fan.' - Eric Meijer.

The 'problem' for (Michael) was he became an England legend before a Liverpool one. He won the hearts of the nation before he won those of the Kop.' - Jamie Carragher.

Two brilliant young strikers inherited by respective Liverpool managers from the youth system; two potentially world class forwards whose Liverpool career (in actual playing time) only briefly overlapped; one utterly embraced by the Kop but his best days were behind him by the age of twenty three, the other, while being admired, always viewed through a slight prism of suspicion and had won the European Player of the Year by the time he was twenty three.

Liverpool supporters are walking exponents of the Chinese curse about living in interesting times, and in the case of Robbie Fowler and Michael Owen we lived through a time that was – for all the shifting sands of change and turmoil – a great time to be a Red, even if it held more than a degree of pain.

There are only two years between the two players but their career trajectory was always going to be radically different. Fowler was viewed by the Kop as one of our own, warts and all, a character carved from the streets of Toxteth, a working class scally who looked slightly bewildered by all the fuss. Owen was a different animal altogether, hailing from a comfortable middle class background, groomed for stardom from a young age. The clean cut and handsome youngster was a marketing man's dream. It would not be exaggerating to claim that if a hypothetical Frankenstein sought to conjure the perfect modern footballer in a laboratory, then the chiselled and athletic visage of Owen would be the result. Robbie was different; Fowler was always different – less a modern Prometheus and more a Jabberwocky of outrageous goalscoring talent. And we absolutely adored him for it.

There was this shrewish and nagging feeling that we didn't actually own Owen. Was he more England's than Liverpool's? Was he finally going to make the long mooted move to one of Europe's giants? Everything about the young star smacked of transience in a red shirt. Given his exploits for Liverpool, there is no doubt that his subsequent tarnished reputation is slightly unfair but, well, the heart loves what the heart loves.

Fowler was the urchin, a Freudian projection onto a football pitch of all of our desires, our dreams of scoring in front of a heaving Kop made incarnate, a flawed but ultimately colourful and three dimensional character.

Michael was the poster boy, dizzying pace and nerveless finishing all wrapped in a pristine package that seemed more contrived than the organic Fowler. Robbie was the Oasis to Owen's Boyzone, the rock star smashing up a stage compared to a Ronan Keating sipping cocoa at home on a Saturday night.

The reality, of course, was not the same and much more complex but there were differing fundamental feelings inspired by both star strikers. The above may be tantamount to glibness but, then, that's football fans.

But this is not to harangue Michael Owen, whose goalscoring exploits should be appreciated and not forgotten. From day one, from the first time he was thrust into the Premiership spotlight by a desperate Roy Evans as Liverpool sought to overcome a two-goal deficit and rescue their title dream, Owen was a prodigious phenomenon. His finish that day against Wimbledon was one that would become synonymous with the youngster; sprint onto a through ball, open body, icily steer the ball into the far corner.

He was seventeen years of age.

Five years previously, the youngster had signed schoolboy terms with Liverpool, despite firm interest from Chelsea, Manchester United and Arsenal; it was Steve Heighway's intervention which had proved decisive as Owen's father, Terry (himself a professional footballer), later claimed:

'(He) wrote us a smashing letter and it was love at first sight for Michael, he was impressed from day one.'

The Chester native then started destroying goal scoring records at Lilleshall (with the FA's School of Excellence) and at youth level with the Reds. In May 1996, nearing the end of a season in which, for the first team, Robbie Fowler was torturing defences up and down the land, Owen scored in the FA Youth Cup Final. Excitement strode the terraces of Anfield and the name of this youngster was whispered up and down the rows of the stadium, in every street and misty Sunday football pitch of the city. Was it possible, did we have a new kid who could be, gulp, even better than Fowler?

The strange dichotomy of the two is apparent in that last sentence. Robbie was twenty one and Liverpool fans were already wetting their lips in anticipation of another virtuoso coming through into the first team.

Fowler, an Evertonian, had seamlessly come through the ranks at Liverpool and had also had his share of hushed whispers from frantically hoping scousers. Roy Evans, who would undoubtedly get the best from young Robbie, had originally seen his future star as an eleven year old banging in a hat-trick against his son, Stephen, in Burscough.

'*Afterwards, I checked that Liverpool had already signed him and fortunately we had*', Evans later recounted.

It was a young Fowler who would provide the only real bright spots as the Souness era began to rapidly unravel.

Ian Rush, writing in his autobiography, claimed that:

'*I saw a lot of the young me in Robbie … I now found myself repeating Phil Neal's advice, telling Robbie to think beyond scoring goals and more about the team and play in general.*'

Rush, the wily old predator, took the young scally under his wing, passing on his instinctive, lateral movement and how to time runs to a willing apprentice. But it wasn't long before this particular apprentice was developing sorcerous traits and by the 1994/95 season, a nineteen year old Fowler was an ever-present in Liverpool's league campaign.

In terms of pure goalscoring talent, Robbie's breakthrough season proved that he was simply peerless (and let's not forget that by the time Fowler was twenty-one, he had broken the thirty goal barrier three seasons in a row. How much would such a player be worth now?).

As John Scales puts it:

'*Robbie was lazy in training. But that's the way strikers are. Ian Rush was the same – Liverpool's all-time leading goal scorer. Maybe Robbie did need to run but he was bursting onto the scene and phenomenally gifted. His finishing ability was the greatest I've seen. Inside the box, outside, headers, the bravery. He had everything, Robbie.*'

Those of us who were lucky enough to witness the coming of God will never forget it. He once said himself:

'*I hate watching live games, no matter who is playing, in case they're 0-0 and boring. You've sat down for an hour and a half and not seen nothing [sic].*'

That was Robbie, goal fixated like any natural striker, but trying to articulate his gifts in his nervous, guttural scouse was beyond him; he could score goals, what was the big deal? That seemed to be the feeling he gave off ('I hate talking about football: I just do it', he once succinctly put it).

And did it he did. Goals from everywhere, a deluge of strikes; head, left foot, right foot, thirty yard volleys, tap-ins, sweeping finishes, adept lobs, bicycle kicks. There was no type of goal beyond the mercurial and precocious forward. As John Williams noted in *Into the Red*:

'Although he wasn't especially quick, he always seemed to have time, even amongst the frenzied action in and around the box; his timing of striking the ball was incredible, he barely scuffed anything with his dinky size sevens, which meant that he could also score startling goals from distance; he also hit the target from any side, frequently taking shots very early on his so-called weaker right foot, and he was also brave and strong in the air; and finally, and biggest attribute of all, Robbie, like Lineker and Solskjaer and only one or two others, somehow 'knew' where the final position of the ball was likely to be whenever it came into the box. No one can teach this: this is vital striker's intelligence.'

In 1995/96, Fowler was at the height of his considerable powers and he scored thirty six goals in all competitions. Robbie – never blessed with much pace – thrived in Evans' patient build up play and wing-back system. His bravery and low centre of gravity meant he often got on the end of crosses (be they zipped along the ground or whipped in high) he had no right to and his uncanny positional sense saw him conjure strikes almost literally from nothing. His second goal against Aston Villa in the 1996 FA Cup Semi-Final graphically attests to this as Robbie gravitated out of the box, almost casually sauntering away from the action, as a corner was delivered by the Reds. Except the cleared ball landed on Fowler's chest and his brilliant, beautiful and sumptuous volley back at Mark Bosnich was simply joyous to behold and Robbie in a nutshell.

The first of what would become a depressing sequence of injuries struck the twenty one year-old striker at the start of the following season; a problem with his back meant that Fowler only scored two goals in the opening eight games. He was in and out of the side throughout that campaign save for one series of matches where he managed to start fifteen games in a row (Robbie scored seventeen times), but 96/97 was less notable for goal scoring than it was two particular incidents that cemented Fowler's legend. The famous protestation at being awarded a penalty after a foul by David Seaman drew praise from no less a figure than Sepp Blatter (insert gag here). A few days later though, the continent's governing body were less impressed when Robbie celebrated a goal against Brann by revealing a T-Shirt in support of striking workers at Liverpool's Bootle Docks. This drew widespread praise from working people everywhere but UEFA – ludicrously – fined Fowler for using football for 'political' ends. A few weeks later, the striker was foolishly sent off in a Merseyside derby, effectively ending his season. With the Reds' form falling off a cliff, Roy Evans turned to one Michael Owen, who didn't disappoint. The strange tale of Robbie and Michael was about to take another twist.

For both strikers – now firmly in the footballing consciousness of a city, the 97/98 season, for vastly different reasons, was a pivotal one and it soon became apparent that the footballing gods were dealing in heavy hands. Robbie was injured again as the campaign kicked off, this time ligament damage keeping him on the sidelines. The young Owen – appearing tiny and nerveless, electrifying and deadly – took his chance in typically assured fashion and was now the focus of attention. Though Fowler intermittently staged comebacks, something was clearly not right and he even managed to get himself sent off for elbowing Leeds United's Per Frandsen in November. Meanwhile, Michael Owen was announcing himself to an entire nation. Following a glut of goals in his debut season by the fresh-faced prodigy, a campaign for Glenn Hoddle to include Owen in his squad for the forthcoming World Cup was gathering pace and a week after he became England's youngest starter of the twentieth century in February, the astonishingly gifted youngster produced a master class of finishing in scoring a hat-trick against Sheffield Wednesday.

Let's be very clear here; it was only after Owen's exploits in France and 'that goal' against Argentina that a cloud of minor suspicion would descend and slightly tamper our affections for the boy-genius. At this juncture, the red half of the city was bouncing at our young star's boundless, fearless optimism and seemingly limitless potential. It was not even seen as hyperbole when *The Liverpool Echo*'s headlines screamed that 'Brazil have Ronaldo, Liverpool, and now England, have Michael Owen.' The reporter went on:

'It's not unreasonable to compare the Reds' young striker with the brilliant Brazilian. Nor is it unreasonable to suggest our man will make any less an impression in the World Cup.

True, Owen does not possess the physical strength which, at the moment, makes Ronaldo the globe's finest player, but he has enough other attributes which, I feel, will one day allow him to inherit his throne.'

This was the level of expectation and heated speculation that the talents of Michael Owen were forging. From Robbie's point of view, at the ripe old age of twenty two, and having scored ninety one goals in one hundred and sixty matches, he had effectively been usurped at his own club by a kid who looked like he had yet to make an acquaintance with a razor blade. And with freakish providence, the end of February was to hold worse for Fowler. In the last few moments of a Merseyside derby the forward collided with Thomas Myrhe and suffered a cruciate ligament injury. Suddenly, catastrophically and just as Michael was eyeing France and a starring role, not only was Robbie's World Cup dream over, but his very career was in jeopardy.

Destiny had apparently decreed that the two brilliant strikers' careers would follow in two radically different tangential arcs. Michael Owen wowed the entire planet at France 1998 while Robbie Fowler sat at home, watching the drama on his TV. And for both forwards, statistically – and given their level of talent – of whom one might normally be expected to come along in a generation, there was more turbulence ahead as their club prepared to change decades of tradition.

For differing reasons, massive question marks now hung over the heads of Liverpool's two star strikers.

CHAPTER 5 - PARTNERING OF THE WAYS

There have been myriad words written about the beginning of the Gérard Houllier regime at Anfield, and in particular, about the dynamics of his relationship with Roy Evans and how the partnership could work. Would it be too much of a stretch to suggest that it was an experiment doomed to failure and that it saved the Liverpool board from making a harsh and painful decision – to dispense with the services of one of their most loyal and well-liked servants? Perhaps, but the impression remains that Liverpool's owners were working in the realms of *realpolitik*; the end would justify the means and if success followed, all would be well. If not, a servant of the club who bled the red of the city, would more than likely fall upon his sword.

Following the recent success of the hitherto unknown Arsène Wenger at Arsenal – a club cast in a similar mould to Liverpool – it was natural that Peter Robinson and the newly arriving Rick Parry (the latter of whom was a confirmed embracer of modernity and had been one of the driving architects of the Premier League) would finally look to the continent to try to get the club back on track. Though the Evans' years had witnessed some sparkling football, the lingering spectres of ill-discipline and a soft underbelly would perhaps need a more authoritarian figure to exorcise them. Moreover, perhaps the fact that sports science, players' diets and analytics were becoming ever more central on the continent might give Liverpool an advantage in a game that was now deadly competitive as the financial rewards continued to spiral. At the very least, it is reasonable to surmise that an outside figure – a break with tradition – might be able to excise the niggling malignancy that was dressing room bad habits.

Peter Robinson was a fan of Houllier and the Frenchman was a fan of the Reds, having fallen in love with the club and the city during his college days in the Sixties. Gérard had actually had a chequered managerial career and had infamously overseen the French national side's late capitulation in their quest to qualify for the 1994 World Cup. But the recent success of *Les Bleus* in the same competition four years later gave Houllier massive kudos as it was he who had sown many of the seeds in French youth football. In short, in the summer of 1998 his stock had never been higher and the disciplinarian and moderniser was mooted as being the perfect tonic for the ills that had beset the Reds.

So, as the sands of football were again shifting during the tumultuous Nineties, Evans accepted that he needed some help. But he was, in fact, under the impression that, as he put it, 'there was a need for something different. The game was turning very European. We spoke to John Toshack…about the idea of appointing a director of football.'

Was the then sole incumbent of the Liverpool manager's job actually unaware of the nature of the job the board had envisioned for the incoming Houllier? Speaking in Simon Hughes' *Men in White Suits*, Roy Evans is adamant and claims that he let his heart rule his head:

'(O)n the football side, we got on. At the end of the meeting, it came to roles, responsibilities and titles. I said something about not having an ego and that I'd do whatever was better for the club. It was a massive mistake. I should have been sharper and brighter … I wasn't strong enough to insist that he would only be a director of football … the board should have known that (two men can't do the same job). It had been tried at other clubs and it hadn't worked.'

There's a discernible sense here of something that could perhaps have been Roy Evans' fatal flaw: a lack of ruthlessness and a desire to accommodate the club he loved so much. His tenure had, after all, hardly been a disaster. But he probably knew his limitations and, typically for such a good and honest human being, wanted what was best for the club. Moreover, he probably knew which way the wind was blowing and that his time was running out. But the appointment of Houllier fatally undermined the Bootle-born boss; there can be no doubt about that and if things went wrong, there could only be one fall guy.

However, despite Evans' misgivings, the new season kicked off with Liverpool in superb form. After defeating Southampton and getting a credible draw against the champions, the Reds travelled to St. James' Park and absolutely destroyed Newcastle. As a beaming Evans and Houllier looked on (together with a grim-faced, newly arrived Ruud Gullit, apparent purveyor – or so he had declared – of sexy football), Michael Owen – fresh from his exploits at the French World Cup and now one of the hottest names on the planet – scored a sizzling hat-trick inside the first fifteen minutes. The image of Owen and Paul Ince, rubbing their hands in metaphorical anticipation of what was in store for the coming season will long live in the memory as the travelling Reds chanted with glee, advising a bemused Gullit what he could do with his 'sexy football'. Liverpool were, according to a Press Association report: 'playing a brand of football that could well become the benchmark for the season.'

Predictably, it was not to last. A defeat at West Ham United followed two games after the Newcastle heroics and, depressingly, the Reds would not win another league game until the 24th October when four goals from every mother's dream son-in-law, Owen, secured the points against Nottingham Forest. But there were more disquieting rumours starting to gather pace; not on a lack of discipline but a lack of unity. As Evans said himself years later:

'it was silly things like what time the bus left – stuff that erodes confidence in the squad. Gérard's a cleverer man than I am, that's for sure. I don't hold any grudges against him but he knew this was going to happen … he was quite happy to bide his time.'

Houllier favoured rotation, Evans, a staunch disciple of Shankly and Paisley, sung from the 'never change a winning team' hymn sheet. There was a dressing room bust up following another insipid 0-0 draw against Valencia in late October and at this stage the writing was not so much on the wall as painted in bright neon-like colours on the stadium terraces: Evans' time was up and the experiment was about to reach its conclusion.

After a dispiriting home defeat to Spurs in a League Cup tie in early November, Roy Evans pulled the plug himself. As John Williams wrote in *Into the Red*, he 'decided that Gérard Houllier needed to pursue his own new direction with the club Evans had loved and served for all of his professional life.' Chairman David Moores and Evans faced a media where there was a tangible air of expectancy; after all, the Sword of Damocles had been practically waiting to fall since Houllier strode into Anfield. The words from the Bootle-born manager were almost anti-climactic and delivered in a close to tearful choke:

'If it's not working, it would be a bigger mistake to stay. I dispute the theory that my time here has been a failure.'

How then, to judge Evans' time in charge? His Liverpool side never finished outside of the top four but, of course, throughout his tenure a finishing position of second and then third was required to qualify for the Champions League. Moreover, he didn't have to contest with a troika of über-rich clubs; Russian oligarchs and Arab billions had yet to arrive. Manchester United may have been approaching the gravy train of wealth that they would become by the time of Evans' successors but, during his time, the disparity of wealth between the two great northern rivals had not yet reached the chasm that it would become. The Premier League was a much more egalitarian landscape, graphically demonstrated by the fact that, in differing seasons, Blackburn Rovers, Nottingham Forest and Newcastle

United all finished above the Reds – despite the latter's relatively high finishes. But Evans helped to bring back a feel-good factor to supporting the Reds; after the grim days of Souness, being talked about as the best footballing team in the country on regular occasions was a breath of fresh air. However, it always seemed like a genuine breakthrough was just around the corner and, sadly, the talented group of footballers that represented the Reds in these years never quite got there.

The indiscipline at the club throughout Roy's time has been discussed already and he and many of the alleged instigators have since made the point that if Liverpool were winning, it wouldn't have mattered. But, as Paul Tomkins has pointed out in *Dynasty*, 'some incidents were contributing to a failure to win trophies.' Drinking was a major problem – something that Houllier would immediately seek to stamp out – but one always had the feeling that Evans was too entrenched in the decades-old British culture of team-building in a pub; the woodwork had been moved dramatically since the Reds' days of success. Alex Ferguson and Arsène Wenger, both seeking to supplant better placed rivals, had shown zero tolerance for any drinking; the former had bombed out the likes of Norman Whiteside and Paul McGrath while the latter bought a cadre of foreign players of huge professionalism that he could trust (while also slinging Paul Merson out of Highbury and playing a huge role in the rehabilitation of Tony Adams). Evans, and this impression is impossible to escape, lacked the ruthlessness to act in a similar manner.

Evans' transfer record must also be taken into consideration and, again, as was highlighted earlier, his biggest signing was also akin to him voluntarily placing his neck on the managerial guillotine. Hindsight may be a wonderful thing, but on such decisions are managerial reputations made and lost. A few years previously, Alex Ferguson had made a similar risky signing with the arrival of Eric Cantona (and the risk was not nearly as expensive) who went on to ignite a generation. Perhaps Roy thought that the complex Collymore may have had a similar effect but the whole situation – despite a decent first eighteen months – rapidly descended into toxicity and corrosiveness. The death knell to dressing room camaraderie was also the harbinger of Evans' Liverpool doom. Roy's successes in the transfer market were steady, Berger probably being the pick of his purchases whilst the likes of McAteer, Scales and Ince had their moments but ultimately flattered to deceive. Phil Babb, after a promising beginning to his Liverpool career, is perhaps remembered more for a collision with the woodwork than for his ability in defence (which is probably a mercy, considering how the final stages of his career in a red shirt went). The high performers during Evans' tenure were players he had inherited or who came through the youth system: McManaman, Redknapp, Fowler and Owen.

But it should be pointed out that Roy Evans managed to steady a ship that was in serious danger of floundering; in some aspects he was the perfect man for the job and he succeeded in reuniting a fractious fan base (not to mention dressing room). His 5-3-2 system came – literally – within an inch of delivering Champions League football and it was a bold and ballsy tactical move. Evans wanted Teddy Sheringham on board in the mid-nineties but was vetoed by the board who thought the Spurs forward was too old (as was, apparently, Marcel Desailly). It's tempting to speculate as to what may have been, particularly when reminded that Sheringham became a Treble winner with Manchester United a few years later (yes, the demands may have been more with the Reds, and he may well have been required to play more games. But given his professionalism, fitness and body type, his legs may not have gone until he was ready for another pitch, to paraphrase Paisley). Evans got the best of Fowler and McManaman and blooded Owen; for that alone, he should be remembered with fondness. In short, he was – and is – a thoroughly decent man who did a reasonably good job in trying circumstances.

In many ways, the transition between the Liverpool of Evans and Houllier coincided with the birth of the truly modern Premier League and, by extension, the truly modern problems that Liverpool would face over the best part of the next two decades. Whereas Evans had been in a position to break the British transfer record with the signing of Stan Collymore, by the time the French manager was wielding Liverpool's cheque book it had – in relative terms to the truly vast financial giant that Manchester United had suddenly become – shrunk considerably. Gérard Houllier, after taking sole charge and being shown graphically the extent of the challenge in the remaining months of the season, was about to embark on a rebuilding programme that would test the Frenchman's international knowledge to the limit.

CHAPTER 6 - FRENCH EVOLUTION

Most people had never heard of the club, let alone the player. Willem II, an obscure Dutch club. A Finnish defender with two 'y's in his surname. There was a collective shrug of the shoulders throughout Liverpool and beyond when Sami signed and a general air of 'who'?

Within a few months, this titan in the heart of the Reds' defence was getting comparisons with legendary stoppers from Liverpool's history.

But – and this has entered Reds' folklore – we were fortunate to get the Finn, and it was not down to Gérard Houllier's extensive European knowledge. Peter Robinson tells the story:

"It was mid-way through the 1998/99 season when there was a knock on the door of my office at Anfield", Robinson said. "I had never met the chap. He came in and introduced himself as a cameraman who covered football in Europe. He knew we were looking for a strong defender and recommended we take a look at Sami, who was playing for Willem, one of the smaller Dutch clubs. That is how it all started. I passed the message on to Gérard and, over the next few months, members of the staff went to Holland to watch him on several occasions."

Hyypiä signed for the Reds on 19th May 1999 for a bargain £2.5 million, and would go on to represent Liverpool with distinction for the next decade, winning everything apart from that elusive Premier League title and writing himself into Anfield mythology.

The signing of the gifted Finn was emblematic of the new Houllier modus operandi; the European model of player, rather than home grown, was now the order of the day. The Liverpool manager – in the summer of 1999, now looking forward to his first season in sole charge – had identified the need to shore up a leaky defence as one of paramount importance if the

Reds were to begin to be rebuilt as a genuine Premier League force. The exuberance and thrilling but ultimately brittle days of Evans' teams would be a thing of the past as the new French manager would implement a counter-attacking style that could be devastating on its day but also have the capacity to veer into sterile territory.

Joining Hyypiä in the heart of defence came Stéphane Henchoz from Blackburn Rovers. The Swiss defender was dependable and resolute, a terrier-like tackler who also possessed a good reading of the game and decent aerial prowess. Like Hyypiä, he also wasn't overly blessed with any great pace but as Houllier's defensive lines tended to be deep, this never caused too many problems. The two would go on to form a formidable partnership over the next few seasons and, despite Gérard's relentless and, to some, irksome rotation, Henchoz and Hyypiä were a constant throughout the early part of his tenure. Protecting the centre-backs was another new arrival, Dietmar Hamann, signed for £8 million from Newcastle United. Despite the relatively high fee, the purchase of the German was still regarded as something of a coup and the unflappable Didi would go on to achieve genuine legendary status in a red shirt.

This triumvirate, who were signed with the express notion of making Liverpool tougher to beat, were also joined by the talented but somewhat lightweight Vladimír Šmicer, the goalkeeper Sander Westerveld and two forwards – Titi Camara and Erik Meijer, both of whom would achieve virtual cult status in their oddly respective ways.

Seven signings then and seven different nationalities; this was, finally, an embracing of the brave new world of English football which was rapidly discarding its previously insular and myopic philosophy. No matter the metric one uses to judge such things, Houllier's first foray into the transfer market was an undoubted success; he acted swiftly and decisively, identifying the players needed to make his vision for the club a reality, sometimes sending his new assistant – the former Liverpool defender, Phil Thompson – throughout the continent on scouting missions. The exacting standards required by Houllier – soon to be felt by the first team squad - ensured a gruelling process for the new number two, as Thompson recounted in his autobiography:

'I can remember flying in and out of Holland watching players, sometimes three times in ten days. I'd set off after training and always be back the next day before the players arrived. I was physically shattered. I can remember lying in bed thinking: Is the manager testing me? Is he checking out my willingness and my loyalty?'

Thoroughness in scouting was now vital to Liverpool as – unlike practically every manager that had managed the club since the days of Shankly – the Reds were no longer dining at the top table of transfer dealings. Whereas Paisley, Dalglish, Souness and Evans had all broken the

British transfer record at some stage, the financial Goliath that Manchester United had become meant that they were operating on a different sphere to the chasing pack. Indeed, Houllier would even find himself financially usurped by Leeds United, as the Yorkshire club began their very own flirtation with monetary Russian roulette; by November 2000, they shelled out a hefty £18 million on Rio Ferdinand while they'd previously spent a combined £13 million on Robbie Keane and Mark Viduka. Manchester United's spending during the first year or so of Houllier's reign was not actually that extravagant (largely owing to the staggering development of some of their youth side), but in the summer of 2001 they could still go and spend £50 million on two players, Ruud van Nistelrooy and Juan Sebastián Verón.

Quite simply, these figures were out of the reach of the Reds. Thompson reckoned that during Liverpool's first window with Houllier in sole charge they had about £12 million to spend. Prudence and casting a bargain-hunting eye near and far would clearly be the order of the day.

The French manager was eager to seize the dressing room and to acquire young players that were malleable enough to be moulded by his ideas; a lofty grasp of professionalism would now be a prerequisite under the new technocrat. Houllier simply wouldn't tolerate any challenge to his authority or those who could conceivably dampen the spirit within the camp.

Paul Ince – self-styled 'Guvnor' and who had perhaps taken the proverbial with the Frenchman's predecessor - was the first to feel the wrath of Houllier and the manager's steely ruthlessness. Ince was popular with the players but due to his ego, stature within the game and previous accomplishments, the potential for the new regime to be undermined from within was overwhelming. Houllier acted swiftly and resolutely and subjected the England midfielder to, as Jamie Carragher put it, 'the most brutal exhibition of management I've seen at Anfield.'

Following a soul-destroying 2-1 defeat to Manchester United in the FA Cup the previous season, during which Ince had hobbled off (with the Reds winning 1-0) only to be fit two days later, the Liverpool captain questioned the training methods of Houllier and Thompson in front of the entire squad.

Houllier's response was as impressive as it was furiously stinging. Carragher takes up the tale:

"'Since the day I arrived, how many five-a-sides have you won?", (Houllier) asked. 'I'll tell you. It's four in six months.' Ince was bewildered, as we all were, by Houllier's grasp of detail. Most players wouldn't remember how many five-a –sides they'd played in a season, let alone how many they'd won or lost. And the manager wasn't

finished. 'Now, maybe you'd like to explain to all the lads what happened to you at Manchester United last week? When my Liverpool team is 1-0 up at Old Trafford in a cup tie, I don't expect my captain to limp off with an injury. If he has to come off the pitch, I expect it to be on a stretcher because he needs to go to hospital in an ambulance.'"

There is almost a Stalinesque show-trials aspect to this anecdote; Houllier, cool, smart and calculated, waiting for an opportunity to show the squad who was actually firmly in control. One can imagine him seizing this opportunity with Machiavellian glee. These were young suggestible players and the manager's robust and imposingly scathing rebuke at having his authority questioned can no doubt have left a serious impression on the squad. As Michael Owen apparently said to Carragher: 'What a manager we've got here'.

In questioning the new manager in public, Ince was effectively, but unknowingly, signing the death warrant on his own Liverpool career; he would be unceremoniously cast off to Middlesbrough within a few months of the incident. Unlike Evans, the nice guy who struggled with the less savoury aspects of authority, the new Liverpool manager was sending out a cast iron signal that he was not to be trifled with. Ince was joined in the Liverpool manager's cull by error prone goalkeeper David James together with the core of Evans' defence: Mark Wright and Jason McAteer (together with Phil Babb at the end of the campaign). A cadre of uninspiring Scandinavians, Stig Inge Bjørnbye, Bjørn Tore Kvarme and Øyvind Leonhardsen also departed, signalling the end of the nineties' flirtation with all things Nordic. Finally, Steve McManaman, to the ire of Reds everywhere, departed for Real Madrid on a Bosman free transfer – the first of its kind in England. But if losing the dribbling and technical skills of the England winger was a blow, then Houllier still had a core of young English talent that he was supplanting with his foreign acquisitions; prodigious goal scoring machine Michael Owen, the ruggedly scouse Jamie Carragher and the clever midfielder Danny Murphy. Soon, a deeply impressive young and lanky local would add to the English heartbeat and announce himself to the world as Steven Gerrard scored on his debut in December of 2000.

Less impressive was the start of the 1999/2000 season. The Reds lost three of their opening six fixtures with the now annual capitulation to Manchester United allayed somewhat by an excellent 2-0 victory over Arsenal at Anfield with Robbie Fowler scoring a magnificent thirty yard strike.

Inconsistency, though, was the watchword for Liverpool as autumn deepened into the frigidity of winter. Yet by Christmas the Reds were, nevertheless, three points off a resurgent Sunderland in the race for the Champions League places (with the league's top three securing qualification).

Though the new year would begin with two back-to-back defeats – one in the league and an FA Cup third round elimination at the hands of Blackburn Rovers – Liverpool finally managed to attain some form and went on a four-month unbeaten run that would only end when Chelsea humbled the Reds 2-0 at Stamford Bridge. But it never got any better for

Liverpool and they limped to the finish line and – from looking certainties to secure Champions League qualification for the first time – this miserable result precipitated a run of five games that would see the Reds fail to score a single goal and collect only two points, resulting in them missing out on third by the same points total. Bradford City hammered home the final nail in Liverpool's coffin of Champions League hopes with an unlikely 1-0 win

on the final day of the season.

Emile Heskey had been signed for £11 million in March, the club bringing the deal forward by a few months as Robbie Fowler continued to struggle with form – his truculence towards the new regime was becoming more and more apparent. Intermittently, the former Leicester City frontman hit the back of the net as the season drew to a close but, ultimately, the Reds goal scoring impetus spectacularly imploded and the final few games of the 1999/2000 season were an uninspired and turgid mess that showed Houllier that, despite some real and tangible progress, there was plenty of work still to do. As Bradford City's manager, Paul Jewell, celebrated a Houdini-like escape from relegation that confirmed the Reds would finish with the UEFA Cup to look forward to the following season, he was probably the only scouser involved in football that wasn't deeply frustrated. But, though no one in the Red camp or the in the bristling and irritated support was to know it, the cloud of missing out on the Champions League had a hugely positive silver lining.

CHAPTER 7 - HERE WE GO GATHERING CUPS IN MAY (AND FEBRUARY)

The 2000/01 was a season when Liverpool announced they were back; a breathless, joyful campaign full of twists and turns, of memorable football and last gasp goals, of celebrating wildly with scarcely believed incredulity.

It was so special because no one – absolutely no one – saw it coming. The naysayers were silenced in a frenzied cacophony of blistering and magical memories; a practical lifetime of them in the space of a few months. Gérard Houllier became a messiah, the most popular manager in a generation, as Reds everywhere – weaned for over a decade on the envy that only those who once had it all and now find themselves cast out can understand – bobbed to the tune of Baha Men's 'Who let the dogs out?'. It was McAllister from forty yards and his manager's beaming, disbelieving and infectious smile; it was winning twice against United and deliriously casting off their hex over us; it was Michael Owen and a brace in Rome; it was Robbie – struggling under the authoritarian nature of the regime – still able to conjure a stupendous twenty yard volley in the first of our Cardiff visits; it was keeping out Rivaldo and company in Barcelona and completing the job at Anfield (can anyone remember the rhythm of our heart beats in those final few moments as an away goal would spell elimination?); it was practical larceny against Arsenal in the FA Cup Final when Owen, like a tartrazine-addled toddler on Christmas morning, all manic eyes and disbelieving smile, tried to summersault after planting past David Seaman with his left foot; it was a deluge of goals, one of them golden, in Dortmund; it was that man Robbie again, somehow scooping an overhead kick into the Charlton goal in the final league game of the season. It was all this and more; a crystallisation of heady joy as the results just kept coming. Sixty three games in four competitions. One hundred and twenty seven goals, three trophies and a return to the promised land of the Champions League.

There've been worse seasons to be a Liverpool supporter.

There was no hint of the special campaign that was to come as Houllier conducted his transfer business with the revolving door policy still ongoing; ten players joined the Reds and eleven left. Save for the arrival of Jari Litmanen in January, none of the dealings of the club were particularly inspiring and the one player that came closest to capturing the imagination of Kopites – Christian Ziege – was, after a long and protracted saga where the Reds were charged with tapping up the German, an unmitigated disappointment. Symptomatic of the seemingly underwhelming nature of Liverpool's incomings was the arrival of a veteran Scot, Gary McAllister. Reds' fans were more than a little sceptical at the acquisition but, like so many that hailed from the Highlands before him, the former Coventry midfielder would go on to paint himself into Liverpool's rich historic tapestry and acted as a catalyst for the glories that were to come. The German defender Markus Babbel also arrived on a free transfer from Bayern Munich. Though not a fantasia signing, it was a canny piece of business – so typical of Houllier at this stage of his Liverpool career – and was actually something of a coup. Babbel would go on to feature prominently in the fantastic campaign we were about to witness. There was something of a faint scandal, much to the bemusement of the French manager, when Nicky Barmby made the trip across Stanley Park to sign for the Reds in a £6 million deal, becoming the first player since Dave Hickson over forty years previously to make the journey. Barmby, a clever, robust and dynamic attacking midfielder, would play his part during the historic season – particularly in Europe.

The campaign kicked off with a routine 1-0 victory at home to Bradford City – the side that had denied the Reds Champions League football on the final day of the previous season. Emile Heskey – brawny in physical stature but seemingly possessed of a fragile ego – scored a thumping winner in a display that would become typical of his Liverpool career. As *The Liverpool Echo* put it:

'Brilliant in one moment, and leaving everyone scratching their heads in bemusement the next.'

Heskey would enjoy a fine campaign as his manager pleaded for patience from a sometimes baying Anfield crowd and unequivocally put his faith in the big striker as the perfect foil for Michael Owen (Robbie Fowler was injured, and though he would return to action soon, he would have a frustrating time of it. Indeed, it would be the end of October by the time

Robbie would start for the Reds).

Heskey thrived on confidence but sometimes this confidence was a very delicate thing; capable of all kinds of goals – lobs, headers, long shots, close range finishes – and a genuine thorn in the side of any defence when on song, too often the forward went missing, particularly as his Anfield career progressed (although it must be noted, this was the only season he played as an out and out striker for the entirety of a campaign and the results weren't half bad).

Fowler was of course a different matter and, clearly, something wasn't right with the darling of the Kop. This deserves some exploration at this stage as the whole Robbie/Houllier dynamic, the offers for the player from other clubs during the campaign, the apparent growing tension behind the scenes, was a major underlying theme of the season's narrative for many in the stands and throughout the Liverpool-supporting world. Relations between the striker and Houllier had been, to say the least, strained for some time. In February 1999, Fowler had indulged in crass, homophobic baiting of Graeme Le Saux and followed this up a few weeks later with the infamous 'cocaine-sniffing' scandal after scoring against Everton. Having been subjected to the familiar 'smackhead' taunts from the Blues' support, the Liverpool forward celebrated his goal by getting on all fours and pretending to sniff one of the painted white lines on the Anfield turf. It was, to be fair to Robbie, witty if ill-advised, but also understandable – to a degree, a gesture made in the spur of the moment. Houllier, in trying to repair the damage, made things worse at his press conference when he, almost surreally, claimed that his striker's actions were a homage to Rigobert Song, the Cameroonian defender who, according to the Liverpool manager, regularly pretended to eat grass – apparently an African custom – after scoring in training. This was naive and cringe-inducing for Houllier, although there should be some sympathy for a manager still new to the scrutiny in the English game and seeking to make excuses for his wayward star (and possibly prevent a ban).

According to Fowler himself, this was the beginning of the end and the reaction from the media to the Reds' boss's excuse sealed the striker's fate; Houllier would, allegedly, never forgive Fowler for being the source of the extreme embarrassment he felt at being a target for the delighted amusement of Fleet Street. In his autobiography, Fowler claimed that a sympathetic (to Robbie) journalist had disclosed:

'It must have been fully two years later when he (Houllier) told a mate of mine how I was finished that day, when he had been ridiculed for defending me … Then he referred back to the 'eating the grass' incident and he let rip. 'I tried to defend your mate, I tried to fucking defend the idiot and what did you do? You ridiculed me. I was made to look ridiculous because of Fowler, and I defended him. I tell you, I will never make that mistake again.'

There is an undercurrent of bitterness in Fowler's autobiography when referring to, as he called the Liverpool boss and his number two, Jekyll and Hyde. Robbie clearly felt he was always being forced out, that he and Jamie Redknapp were the last of the Spice Boys, a legacy of an era of ill-discipline and that he was fighting a losing battle from the day the French manager walked in. But Fowler's injury problems were compounded by alcohol (indeed, Houllier, famously averse to the demon drink, directly blamed his striker's fitness problems on over-indulgence. According to Jamie Carragher, the Liverpool boss thought even an ultra-professional like Roy Keane could be improved by abstinence; Fowler, caught up in nights out and rows with bouncers, was clearly doing himself no favours given the nature of the new authoritarian regime).

Moreover, Robbie's claim that Houllier and Thompson did more harm than good – at this juncture – as they set about dismantling a 'fantastic young squad', just does not wash. Fowler alleged that Houllier got rid of some players too early and destroyed a side with massive potential:

'Houllier got rid of Jamo, Incey, Trigger, Harky, Jason McAteer, Mark Wright, Phil Babb, Karlheinz Riedle [sic], Tony Warner, Stig Bjornebye, Bjorn Kvarme and Oyvind Leonhardsen overnight and then completed the job by bombing out Steve Staunton, Brad Friedel, Vegard Heggem and such good young players as Dominic Matteo, David Thompson, Stephen Wright and, eventually, Jamie Redknapp and me.'

It's hard to escape the notion that Fowler is guilty of that most human of emotions: fear and aversion to change. There were more than a few reasons to get rid of all of the above: dwindling form, injury, ageing, insufficient quality, and undermining the management (or all five in the case of some).

It could well be a quirk of timing that led Robbie and his manager down the road of antipathy from which, ultimately, Fowler would have no escape. Houllier, for example, got to Jamie Carragher before bad habits had truly set in and turned the defender's career around. Was Robbie just a little too entrenched in being the star youngster, the darling of Anfield, for whom it all came so naturally and who had, for years, not completely treated his body in a manner befitting of a modern professional footballer? Houllier was never going to tolerate this and was right in constantly reminding his wayward star on the perils of alcohol. Perhaps, the ultimate tragedy for Fowler was that he was born ten years too early or ten years too late to become the absolute legend that his talent deserved. Like many of his peers, Robbie straddled the defining moments of two vastly differing eras.

So Fowler was always going to struggle in this historic campaign and had, in reality, done so for a few seasons at this stage. Bad luck played its part but – and this is by Robbie's own admission – so did poor decisions such as the time he was dropped for the final game of the 99/00 season when Bradford City denied the Reds a Champions League berth. Fowler, after being given permission to attend a family event, and after seeing the 1-0 reversal (with more than a few units of alcohol on board), decided it would be a good idea to ring the manager:

'So I rang him and this time I left a message. It was short and to the point:

"I'm gutted you cost me the Champions League. I hope you're fucking satisfied in leaving me out now."'

One can imagine that this didn't go down too well with the management. Nevertheless, Fowler was again given another chance and knew this was it; he would need to knuckle down, get back in shape – fully – and embrace the philosophy and ethos of his manager. Typically though, disaster struck during a pre-season game essentially meaning – due to all of these factors and more – that arguably Liverpool's greatest and most natural finisher ever would be a bit-part player during one of the club's most successful seasons. For Robbie, there was a Dickensian twist to a campaign that would yield so much for his beloved club, it was the best of times and the worst of times and as Fowler said himself:

'It was a schizophrenic season for me. In terms of trophies, I have never had a better year, and it is unlikely to be matched by very many people. In terms of my mental state, it got worse and worse as the season wore on.'

For the Liverpool squad as a whole, there was a bipolar nature to proceedings; following Heskey's winner against Bradford City, the Reds would get beaten by Arsenal fairly comprehensively before drawing against Southampton after being three goals ahead with fifteen minutes left. Though Liverpool settled down and started churning out results, there was always a sense of slight mistrust in watching the side; a 3-0 reverse to Chelsea was followed by a 4-0 thumping of Derby County with Heskey scoring his first senior hat-trick. The Reds were, in a nutshell, and before Christmas, consistent only in their inconsistency. After beating Olympiacos 2-0 in the UEFA Cup in early December, Liverpool then went down 1-0 at Anfield to George Burley's newly promoted Ipswich Town (the Scottish manager was on his way to a Manager of the Year award that was frankly ludicrous given Houllier's achievements. Apparently the domestic game hadn't quite learned to embrace all things continental).

But it was about to get a whole lot better as the festive season beckoned. A week after the Tractor Boys humbled the Reds, Liverpool made the trip to Old Trafford, a ground that had not been a happy hunting one for years. Danny Murphy's impeccable free kick gave the Reds a 1-0 victory and Liverpool followed up this brilliant result with a 4-0 hammering of Arsenal with Fowler finally igniting with a ninetieth minute goal after coming off the bench. *The Guardian* may have claimed that it was, as the headlines noted piercingly, 'Houllier's new dawn', but the French manager was not getting carried away, given the relatively poor start to the campaign:

'I don't think Manchester United will drop ten points in the second half of the season. I still regret that we are possibly five or six points short if we are to have a run at the Champions League. Even if we have beaten them, it doesn't mean that we are at Manchester United's level. We are not. But this team will get better in the second half of the season.'

But even Houllier could not have envisaged the degree of his team's improvement in the campaign's second half. Indeed, following the victory over Arsenal, the Reds would only suffer defeat in all competitions on five more occasions – out of a total of thirty five games. This squad was evolving, improving and developing before our eyes. Westerveld – though still prone to the occasional concentration lapse (he was a Liverpool 'keeper, after all) – gave the defence confidence and was an excellent shot stopper; Hyypiä and Henchoz's defensive axis was watertight as they complemented each other and would sweat blood for the cause; Babbel was superb at right-back, solid but also a great attacking outlet; Jamie Carragher, after starting the campaign on the bench and then tried in midfield, would make the left-back slot his own; Hamann was a rock in shielding his defence, stalking the defensive third of the pitch, effortlessly breaking opposition probes and sweeping up with canny authority; Steven Gerrard was showing the talent and drive that would see him develop into a world class midfielder; Danny Murphy weighed in with crucial goals and was a clever, incisive passer: Barmby and Berger could be relied upon to find the net and offer attacking nous; the newly arrived Finnish superstar, Jari Litmanen, offered guile and adroit technical knowhow; Emile Heskey was having the season of his life and dovetailed brilliantly with his striking partner, Michael Owen, as the latter finished the season with an absolute bang on the way to winning European Footballer of the Year. Robbie Fowler, new signing Igor Biscan and Christian Ziege also made telling contributions. Jamie Carragher called it the best Liverpool team he ever played in (although this was just prior to Rafa's monolithic 2008-09 vintage). It was a side brimming with character, big players, strength, technical ability, pace and ambition.

Then there was Gary McAllister. It's hard to mention the Scot's influence on this campaign without referencing the hideous cliché about aging like a fine wine. But to stretch the metaphor, McAllister was like opening a bottle of fine vintage at a table and letting it breathe until the food arrived. By the time the four course meal that was the Treble and Champions League qualification was served, the wine was fulsome, integral and vital to the whole experience. McAllister became a symbol of the unlikely nature of the entire season, and emblematic of the magic of the club, a player in the autumn of his career writing himself into Anfield mythology in the space of a few short months.

And what a few months they were; a gasping, variegated, gorgeous, seemingly endless parade of two matches a week, of lacerated nerves, of moments imprinted on the collective consciousness of an entire fan base. Of cheering and of having fun. Of barely believing what was going on in front of our eyes.

Pick your memory:

There was Michael Owen defying the odds and finishing brilliantly twice in Rome; the striker at the very peak of his predatory prowess. The return leg wasn't exactly conducive to a steady heartbeat as the referee awarded Roma a penalty with the Italians 1-0 ahead on the night and then inexplicably changed his mind.

Then there was Robbie's partial redemption in Cardiff in the League Cup Final as he let fly with a twenty yard lobbed half volley that sailed over Ian Bennett in the Birmingham City goal for an early lead. But, in what would be symptomatic of the entire season, we didn't do it the easy way and, following a late equaliser, were put through the nerve shredder of penalty kicks, finally emerging victorious when Sander Westerveld saved from Andy Johnson.

Manchester United were beaten comprehensively in the league in late March, an extraordinary long range missile from a rapidly maturing Steven Gerrard and an adept finish from Fowler giving the Reds a 2-0 victory. Sandwiched between two UEFA Cup semi-final epics was the 3-2 win over Everton at Goodison; an astonishing extravaganza of a match, a see-sawing rollercoaster that was settled in the ninetieth minute as Gary McAllister's disguised forty yard free kick crept in at Paul Gerrard's near post. The home leg of the aforementioned UEFA Cup Semi-Final saw Anfield return to the halcyon days of yore, all cacophonous noise and banner waving, the pitch drenched in the floodlit magic that had been gone for too long. A first half penalty from that man McAllister (hit past a future Liverpool goalkeeper, Pepe Reina) gave the Reds a tenuous 1-0 aggregate lead; a goal for Barcelona would spell elimination for Liverpool. Nerves jangled and stomachs heaved as we held out for our first European final since 1985, and Heysel.

Now came the summer. May dawned with the realisation that we had two cup finals to look forward to but also, for the league campaign to end in qualification for the Champions League, we would probably have to take maximum points from our remaining four fixtures. Were we being greedy, graspingly hankering over a top three finish when the season had already been so memorable and promised more? Undoubtedly, but that is football fans, we want it all.

And, in one memorable, remarkable month, we got it.

Michael Owen and Gary McAllister scored the goals in a 2-0 victory over Bradford City that saw the Reds leapfrog Ipswich Town and Leeds

United into that all important third spot (Houllier had said throughout the cup runs that the campaign was all about qualification for UEFA's flagship; anything else would be viewed as anti-climactic if Liverpool failed in this pursuit). Four days later, Newcastle United were put to the sword, a brilliant hat-trick from Owen securing a 3-0 victory at Anfield. The England striker was coming into impressive form at just the right time and put it concisely when he told *The Guardian*:

There's an air of confidence here now, but all our success is just potential at the moment. If the season stopped now we'd consider it to have been very good, but it could yet be brilliant – a season that no one dreamt of at the start of the year.'

A 2-2 draw with Chelsea on the 8th May left many nervous; twice the Blues came from behind to ensure that the Reds would now have to beat Charlton Athletic on the final day of the league campaign to guarantee Champions League football for the following season. This effectively meant that Liverpool would now face three cup finals in the space of seven days.

Cardiff's Millennium Stadium beckoned first; a gloriously hot Saturday afternoon, the FA Cup Final template writ large in blue skies and a gorgeous green pitch, the terraces heaving, a sea of red and white. Arsenal could – and should – have been out of sight before Freddie Ljungberg gave them a seventy second minute lead. Surely there was no way back now, surely the biggest week in Liverpool's recent history was going to get off to a depressing start? Combining flair with steel, this was a formidable Arsenal side with Vieira, Thierry Henry, Robert Pirès and the goal scorer, Ljungberg, all at their peak. As John Williams wrote in *Into the Red*:

'Okay, let's get real; this is now officially over. We have shown little. And deserve less, and we have yet to come back from a goal down in the whole of the 2000-01 league campaign, let alone against these accomplished and experienced misers in a major final … so this begins to feel like the emptiness of the 1996 'spice boys' Liverpool FA Cup final loss against United, another major occasion when we simply failed to turn up.'

Houllier took off Šmicer for Fowler and brought on Patrick Berger for Danny Murphy but still Liverpool huffed and puffed. There is no way back here, we thought. None. Let us be put out of our misery; the writing has been on the wall from the first few minutes; Vieira has played through the young pretender, Steven Gerrard, and Henry has, with feline grace, toyed with Henchoz. But, improbably, magically, a free kick from Gary Mac and a swivel from Owen and we are level. Out of nowhere, we are level with these aristocrats of passing and authority. They couldn't finish us off; we refused to wilt in the sun, and suddenly the entire mood and dynamic shifts. There is an air of inevitability as five minutes later, Berger hits a ball towards a scampering Michael Owen. Adams and Dixon are favourites to get there but our little England striker outstrips them and with his left foot steers an unerring arrow past Seaman. From the moment the ball leaves Owen's foot, we know it's in and we have robbed this fine Gunners side of the FA Cup. There is no guilt, only exhilaration as vice-captain Robbie and the perennially injured club captain, Jamie Redknapp, together with the colossus Sami, lift the trophy.

A few short days later, most of us having barely recovered and still practically bronchial, the Reds were off to the *Westfalenstadion* in Dortmund. The opponents were the Spanish side, Alavés, and a low scoring, cagey affair was confidently and sagely predicted by most. Nine goals later, extra time and a Golden Goal and, again, shortness of breath was a malady felt by all. It was an epic European final, one that, for excitement and drama, would only be outdone by events in Istanbul four years later. The match had initially looked like being a formulaic affair as goals from Markus Babbel and Steven Gerrard had given the Reds a 2-0 lead by the sixteenth minute. Iván Alonso pulled a goal pack but, after Owen was pulled down in the box, McAllister restored Liverpool's two goal advantage from the spot. Half-time offered some respite and Kopites felt secure and satisfied with how the game had gone. Six minutes into the second half and it was 3-3 as Javi Moreno scored twice. This was now another exercise in palpitations and fluctuating blood pressure, as the game ebbed and flowed with both sides showing impressive attacking intent. Robbie then entered the fray and scored a magnificent slaloming fourth that was surely the winner in the seventy third minute. But this incredible season had more twists for Kopites and with the clock ticking down, with whistles starting to mingle and merge in the stands, Jordi Cruyff headed the Spanish side level. Extra time then, as the emotional wringer tightened. Owen had been substituted and now the Reds missed his pace and the outlet he supplied; the game had become a war of attrition, a game of chicken and we watched on, grim-faced, to see who would blink. With less than a minute left and after sitting through thirty minutes of gut-wrenching torture, Delfí Geli inadvertently headed a Gary McAllister free kick past his own keeper. The stadium erupted but the players seemed unsure; it was probably the reaction of the fans that reminded those on the pitch wearing red that they had won the UEFA Cup by a Golden Goal.

The season wasn't over yet. Three cups had been secured but still confirmation on qualifying for that elusive Champions League waited for us. There had to be a sting in the tail, footballing campaigns were surely not this memorable and glorious. Charlton Athletic gave their all in the first half of the final game of this marathon of a season but once Robbie Fowler had put the Reds in front with a stupendous piece of impudent improvisation, there was only going to be one outcome. The game finished 4-0 and Liverpool fans were left to reflect on the momentous achievement and staggering few months that they had been privileged to witness.

CHAPTER 8 – HEARTBREAK

October 13th 2001: Liverpool Football Club faced Leeds United at Anfield in what would turn out to be a fairly uneventful 1-1 draw. Events off the pitch, however, were anything but routine. Gérard Houllier, the Reds' new messiah, the man who had brought back the glory days a few short months ago, was about to have a date with destiny that had nothing to do with football. That cold afternoon, as his side came back from a goal down against the then league leaders, the Reds manager diced with mortality and came out the other end…but only just. The impact of the aortic dissection that Houllier suffered and the severity of it should not be underplayed. Perhaps, close to a subconscious level, we have all understated what struck that Saturday but, for the record, here's what a heart surgeon had to say on the matter at the time:

'Death can occur at any time from the moment the tear occurs: it could be hours, days, weeks or months. It can also lead to heart attacks and stroke, and to a cut off in the supply of blood to limbs which can be fatal, too … During surgery, the patient is kept on a heart-lung machine which their blood goes into. Here it is oxygenated and put back into the patient. The machine takes over from the heart and lungs, so that we can stop the heart beating and the patient stays alive … In order to do that, we cool the patient down to 14 or 15 degrees C (normal body temperature is 37 C). It takes about one to two hours to do this, and an hour more to warm them again after surgery. In these hypothermic temperatures when the brain is asleep, the body's demand for oxygen is reduced so that it can tolerate a period of about 20 minutes when it has no blood supply at all. That is enough time for us to do the work that we need to.'

The Grim Reaper was not so much knocking at Houllier's door as breaking and entering. The Liverpool manager went through an eleven-hour operation with much of the footballing world unaware of just how serious the problem was. By Sunday morning however, it became very clear that if the French manager was ever to return, it would be months and not weeks.

Liverpool fans were reeling but there was more drama and angst in store for us: six weeks later, Robbie Fowler left for Leeds United, in a move that was sanctioned by Houllier from his hospital bed. But if the manager's heart problems were a veritable bolt from the blue, the sale of God – though heartbreaking in itself – was a slow burner. Quite simply, this eventuality had been coming from the moment the Liverpool manager first walked into Anfield. In November 2001 Houllier, fresh from delivering three trophies and a return to the Promised Land of Champions League football, would never have a better opportunity to rid himself of a player who, though he may have admired, ultimately was a source of huge frustration. The manager's flirtation with death – and the fact that this heightened our affection for him – added to the sense of 'now or never' for the Reds' sometimes wayward striker.

Even before the season kicked off, there had been a sense of inevitability about Fowler's eventual transfer. A training ground spat between the striker and Phil Thompson a few days before the Charity Shield match with Manchester United had resulted in Robbie being banished from the first team. In their respective autobiographies, the two predictably have different accounts of what happened on the training pitch but Jamie Carragher, speaking to *Four Four Two* in 2010 said:

'Robbie was having some shots at the goal, and Phil was getting some balls out. Robbie wasn't trying to hit him but wanted to give him a scare and got very close. Robbie was laughing and Phil went mad. Robbie wasn't in the team and was probably up for a fight with anybody at the time. Both went toe-to-toe for a bit but soon calmed down.'

The clock was ticking on Fowler's Liverpool career and though no-one could claim that the striker was an innocent victim, it's hard not to come to the conclusion that, like Ince before him, there was more than a whiff of show trials about the whole incident. Houllier wanted rid of Fowler; there can be no doubt about it and he seized on the opportunity that this snowballing furore gave him. The Frenchman saw the Scouser as disruptive and never far away from either injury, suspension or scandal; he was one of the few still remaining at the club from the Evans era and, moreover, one can imagine Robbie's massive popularity with the adoring Kop irking the sometimes egotistical Houllier. The Liverpool manager preached the team ethos, a collective mentality and so we can only speculate as to how much Fowler's name being sung as he warmed up annoyed Houllier. But the reality is that Fowler – never the quickest but now shorn of even more pace due to injury and a striker who thrived on low passes across the box – was simply the wrong type of player for the system employed by the Liverpool boss. Short of Leeds United winning the league with their new acquisition firing them along the way, in November 2001 Houllier couldn't really lose. The Frenchman's legacy may have been ultimately tarnished in the long run by his treatment of Robbie, but when the transfer went through there was a stoic acceptance from Reds' fans that it may be for the best (and, to be fair, save for a brief period at the beginning of his career in Yorkshire, Fowler never really got close to resurrecting the form that had made him something akin to a deity to so many).

Robbie Fowler's last few games for Liverpool Football Club were a microcosm of his career under the Frenchman. As his manager recuperated and Phil Thompson took over managing the squad, Fowler hit a hat-trick in an emphatic 4-1 win over Leicester City at Filbert Street. He was then almost exclusively used as a substitute for the next month before an ignominious final game in the red of Liverpool as he was hauled off in the 46th minute against Sunderland following a Dietmar Hamann red card. Two days later he was a Leeds United player.

Christmas beckoned with Liverpool's manager picking the team from hospital, one of the fans' favourite ever players departing and the death of one of the city's beloved sons with George Harrison succumbing to cancer. Nevertheless, a 2-1 victory over Aston Villa on Boxing Day saw the Reds just three points behind the league leaders, Newcastle, in third. New signing Jerzy Dudek – signed, along with Chris Kirkland, following a calamitous mistake by goalkeeper Sander Westerveld – was looking like an inspired purchase; Michael Owen was thriving in the system and would finish the season with twenty eight goals (and the Balon D'Or); Danny Murphy was making good on his early promise – a scorer of vital goals and an incisive and hard working professional; Steven Gerrard continued his astonishing development and then there was the athletic dynamism of another new signing, John Arne Riise. Nicolas Anelka joined on loan from PSG on the 20th December: pacey and strong with a cold eyed lethality on his day, the former Arsenal star looked the real deal during his brief stay at Anfield but Houllier ultimately decided that he was not for Liverpool, a baffling decision and one that will be discussed in due course.

Any hints that there would be a dichotomy between a pre and postoperative Gérard Houllier were very far from all Reds' minds when the Liverpool manager made his long awaited comeback in March. The scene was set for one of those special, shiver-inducing Anfield nights as the Reds took on Roma in the Champions League, needing a two goal win to progress to the knockout stage. It was one of those occasions when we, as fans, realise how much of a privilege it is to support Liverpool. A mosaic in the Kop welcomed the manager back and as Houllier was greeted by Fabio Capello in a warm embrace, the atmosphere was building to an electric crescendo. Jari Litmanen gave the Reds an early lead, icily keeping his cool from the penalty spot in a flag waving cauldron. The fairy tale ending was completed when Emile Heskey rose to plant a towering header past Francesco Antonioli in the Roma goal. The Anfield eruption – and the sheer adoration felt for the manager – at the final whistle was an almost anachronistic flashback to the halcyon days of Saint-Étienne; that night in early 2002 was certainly comparable to most in Liverpool's illustrious European history.

Phil Thompson, who had ably managed the Reds as Houllier recovered, summed up the buoyancy in the air as Liverpool welcomed back their manager in victory:

'It was a fantastic night, as good as anything I have witnessed. There were incredible scenes in the dressing room and it was tremendous knowing that we had not only taken a further step in the Champions League, but fulfilled our pledge to ensure we were still involved when Gerard returned.'

The Reds were indeed still in Europe's premier competition and it was a noteworthy achievement to have qualified for the quarter-finals in Liverpool's return to the competition after a sixteen year hiatus. Bayer Leverkusen awaited the Reds and Houllier – perhaps still understandably flushed from the Roma epic, or perhaps showing a nascent hubristic streak that would begin to manifest itself over the next couple of seasons – declared that the club were 'ten games from greatness'. Hindsight showed it to be a brash statement, but it looked like a tantalisingly real prospect. After a last minute winner from Vladimír Šmicer gave Liverpool a 1-0 win over Chelsea, the Reds found themselves top of the Premier League, a point above Manchester United and two clear of Arsenal (although the Gunners – ominously and menacingly – had two games in hand).

The Germans arrived at Anfield for the first leg of the Champions League Quarter-Final; the prize not only a place in the last four, but a potentially epic, ecstatic or heartbreaking, tie with Manchester United. Leverkusen may have played in a pragmatic, functional way (much like their opponents on the night) but this was a formidable unit, sprinkled with genuine star dust in the shape of Michael Ballack, Dimatar Berbatov, Zé Roberto and Oliver Neuville. Sami Hyypiä gave the Reds a narrow one goal advantage but the real test was to come in the return leg in the BayArena a week later. It was another momentous clash, full of drama and goals, but ultimately ended in crushing despair for the Reds. Michael Ballack had given the Germans the lead on the night only for Abel Xavier – recently signed on a free transfer from Everton – to equalise just before half time. Leverkusen now needed to score twice and Liverpool fans prematurely – but understandably given the miserly nature of Houllier's side – started planning for the Battle of Britain that would be the semi-final. However, in five minutes midway through the second half, the Germans scored twice, for the first time putting them ahead in the tie. Hollow, disbelieving anguish was felt by Reds everywhere until in the seventy eight minute, Jari Litmanen slalomed his way through a packed box and passed the ball past Hans-Jörg Butt into the net. A glorious goal seemed to have put us one step closer to glory only for Lucio, Leverkusen's Brazilian defender, to be put through six minutes later, and finish between Dudek's legs. Another epic European encounter ended in heartbreak for Liverpool on a night when the icy finishing of Michael Owen (who missed three one-on-ones) and the pragmatic paucity of the back line – the constants on which the previous eighteen months had been built – deserted the Reds. There were also the first whisperings of disapproval from the Liverpool supporters who had been baffled by Houllier's decision to take off Hamann for Šmicer in the sixty first minute and with the score 1-1 on the night. FIve minutes later it was 3-1. The Liverpool manager defended his decision – and again, hindsight is a wonderful thing – but, at the very least, this showed a troubling, embryonic fallibility in a manager who had previously been practically bullet-proof.

After the crushing nature of the defeat in Germany, the Reds rallied – to a degree – and routinely beat Sunderland and Derby County in their next two games. However, Arsenal just kept on winning and the Gunners were a gargantuan, uber-talented and ruthless side – a perfect marriage of skill and steel and blessed with footballers playing at the peak of their formidable powers. Liverpool relinquished top spot in the Premier League to Arsène Wenger's charges following a 1-0 defeat to Spurs and that was it. Arsenal made no mistake in the run in and coasted to the league title. Liverpool finished a hugely credible second – above Manchester United for the first time in a decade – and that elusive first Premier League now felt tantalisingly close.

It was with a strange mixture of pride and regret, of optimism tinged with ruefulness, that Liverpool supporters prepared to take a break from the ceaseless drama of supporting Liverpool Football Club. But as we looked to the east for the forthcoming World Cup, little did we know that, for Houllier, this was as good as it would get.

CHAPTER 9 - JUDGING HOULLIER

The summer of 2002 was, for many Liverpool supporters, when things began to unravel for Gérard Houllier. Three signings stand out as the apogee of poor talent spotting and most probably give Reds a headache nearly fifteen years later when this was written.

We were meant to kick on, we were meant to take the final step, the gradual improvement was supposed to reach its glorious zenith with that much sought after league title. Not for the first time, we were to be severely disappointed.

El Hadji Diouf, Salif Diao, Bruno Cheyrou; a depressing troika of underachievement and a trio that have – rightly or wrongly – come to symbolise the massive displacement between the Houllier that came before his health issues and the Liverpool manager after he had almost died. It may be overly simplistic – in fact it almost certainly is – but the transfer dealings in the summer of 2002 were a massive alarm bell, something which became progressively clearer with every passing month.

Liverpool had signed Diouf after passing up the chance of securing the permanent signature of Nicolas Anelka - another decision that had many supporters scratching and shaking their heads. From the outside this made little sense, but the Liverpool management had been privy to some disturbing (and, it has to be said, typical) noises from the French striker's camp. Apparently there had been an attempt from Anelka's agents to sell him back to Arsenal and, as Phil Thompson noted:

'It told us a lot about the advice he was getting (which) had caused issues at other

clubs and we didn't want to take any chances.'

Steven Gerrard, who would soon don the mantle of captain as his manager sought desperately to turn things around, was scathing in his assessment of Diouf, who he claimed was the signing by the Reds that he liked least. In his autobiography, Gerrard wrote:

'It seemed to me that Diouf had no real interest in football and that he cared nothing about Liverpool Football Club. For example, the way he spat a huge globule of gunky phlegm at a Celtic fan ... summed up his contemptuous and spiteful demeanour ... the only positive aspect of the otherwise ugly signing is that he worked hard on the pitch ... but after a while I decided Diouf simply wasn't your usual footballer. It seemed to me as if football got in the way of his social life.'

Jamie Carragher was equally unimpressed with the Senegalese forward:

'In all my years at Anfield, I've never met a player who seemed to care less about winning or losing. An FA Cup defeat at Portsmouth in February 2004 effectively sealed Houllier's fate months before his sacking, and there was a desolate scene at Melwood the following day. No one was more distressed than Mo (Owen), who'd missed a penalty at Fratton Park. As he arrived at the training ground with his head down, Diouf drove in with his rave music blaring out of his car, then danced his way across the car park into the building ... his attitude disgusted me.'

Nor was Carragher impressed by Diouf's ability on the footballing pitch claiming that 'after a few training sessions with (him), I'd have walked to Man City to get Anelka back.'

Bruno Cheyrou was simply, and admittedly with the benefit of hindsight, a bewildering signing. He lacked both the pace and the physicality to thrive in the fast-paced English game and equally baffling was his new manager's assertion that he could be the new Zinedine Zidane. This was ill-advised and a troubling indication of where the manager was heading; strange, inexplicable utterances would increasingly become the currency that the formerly formidable Houllier now dealt in.

Then there was Salif Diao, who Carragher, perhaps slightly unkindly, deemed a 'catastrophe'. The assessment of the Liverpool defender on his new team mate was contemptuous and scathing in the extreme: '(H)e couldn't pass, was a liability when he tackled, and never looked like scoring a goal. And they were his good points.' Though this may be a mite unfair, the thoughts of the two Liverpool stalwarts on the signings that summer speak volumes and point to the fact that the first burgeoning notions that their manager may be losing his powers were taking hold. If managers live and die by their transfer record, then the signing of this trio of players was akin to Houllier tying a noose around his own neck. Just for the record, the Reds also signed Patrice Luzi and Alou Diarra and if this duo aren't as notorious as the aforementioned terrible three in Liverpool fans collective consciousness, it's only because they barely featured for the first team.

In terms of results, Houllier's third season in sole charge began with a hugely impressive run; it would be November before the Reds suffered their first defeat in the Premier League. But performances were worrying, and though some supporters speculated as to how good this team could be when they clicked, the reality was that Liverpool had been lucky with results and when the wheels fell off following a 1-0 defeat to Middlesbrough at the Riverside, they did so spectacularly. This fixture was like a harbinger, an awakening to the reality that this squad of players was actually poor. Astonishingly, given the progress thus far in Houllier's reign, the Reds would not win another league game until Emile Heskey gave Liverpool victory over Southampton near the end of January.

The Champions League campaign had been similarly depressing; indeed, unlike the domestic season, the Reds never really got going. A certain Rafa Benítez dished out a footballing lesson with his superbly orchestrated Valencia side and the Swiss side Basel effectively condemned the Reds to the UEFA Cup by snatching two draws. Liverpool would then be eliminated in this competition by Celtic in the fifth round in a tie that became infamous due to the spiteful spit of disgraceful Diouf.

The league campaign limped on with Houllier not even able to find solace in a previously miserly defence. The hitherto unflappable Polish goalkeeper, Jerzy Dudek, was struck down with a serious case of Liverpool goalkeeper malady and rapidly lost confidence as the season progressed; he would find himself rotated with the young Chris Kirkland but did manage an inspired performance in the League Cup Final as the Reds salvaged some crumb of comfort with a 2-0 victory over Manchester United. But by the end of the campaign, Liverpool's great rivals finished nineteen points ahead of the Reds who now found themselves languishing in fifth place and confined to the UEFA Cup. Chelsea, soon to be bankrolled by Russian billions, took the place of the Reds at Europe's top table; we didn't know it at the time, but theirs would now be a vice-like grip on a top four place, plunging more doubt upon an already panic-stricken Liverpool support.

If the fan base was agitated, Houllier seemed in the midst of full on paranoia. Never the type to take well to criticism, and having previously worn a bullet-proof vest against the potential barbs of the media thanks to his initial success, the dramatic downturn in form and the subsequent reproach left the manager in a cloud of bemusement and befuddlement, hinting darkly at what he viewed as a campaign against him by former players. A slew of statistics was routinely trotted out to try to mask his team's shortcomings and the previous urbanity and managerial aloofness which he had made his own was now replaced by a haunted visage. At press conferences, Houllier's eyes darted here and there as he became a walking caricature of uncertainty and frustration. As the 2003/4 season dawned, many were of the opinion that he should do the honourable thing and fall on his sword, but still others thought that the previous campaign was merely a blip and that the Liverpool manager could recapture previous assurance. But the hovering and troubling spectre of his illness was never far from any Liverpool supporter's thoughts; had Gérard Houllier lost that vital spark, that essential extra couple of percent that separate the good from the very good? The footballing landscape was shifting dramatically again with the astonishing millions being pumped into Chelsea by Roman Abramovich; at the very least there was a sense that the French manager was now ill-equipped to face this additional challenge.

As Paul Tomkins previously observed, the ill-advised splurge in the summer of 2002 meant there was little funding available for reinforcements in 2003. Harry Kewell was the latest so-called coup that the Reds secured but, after a decent start to his Anfield career, he faded in a haze of injuries and poor form. Anthony Le Tallec and Florent Sinama-Pongolle had long been identified as 'gems' by Houllier and finally arrived but neither made the grade (although the latter made a contribution on the road to Istanbul). Only Steve Finnan, signed from Fulham for £3.5 million, could be termed a good signing and this was effectively what spelt Houllier's doom: one player succeeded out of a total of eleven signings made between 2002 and 2004. The contrast between the Liverpool manager's first forays into the transfer market, when Hyypiä, Hamann, Babbel, McAllister et al. had arrived, and the newer recruits was stark indeed.

There was a perplexing cloud of inertia swirling around the Liverpool side throughout Houllier's last campaign at the helm; results were resolutely inconsistent, but arguably worse, the performances were usually stilted and unconvincing. Emile Heskey's confidence had completely deserted him, Biščan and Diao were sometimes played in central defence, Owen looked like his mind was already in Madrid, Danny Murphy – previous supplier of vital goals – now found himself frequently rotated, Dudek struggled, his personal nadir that was a litany of calamitous mistakes in the previous season now casting a palpable cloud over him, Šmicer and Kewell frustrated and perplexed. The twin scouse bright spots that were Carragher and Gerrard appeared suffocated by the pall that had settled over the club. Liverpool somehow managed to finish fourth – which showed the weakness of the league, just before a golden age for English clubs in Europe – but finishing in a Champions League place could not disguise the troubling ineptitude and underwhelming nature that the Reds habitually displayed. With Liverpool thirty points behind the new champions, Arsenal, and with fans now joining in the incessant tide of criticism from the media – who had started to question Houllier's sanity as well as his suitability for the job – the time had come for a change and in May 2004, he left the club.

How, then, to judge Gérard Houllier? Though often dismissed as the 'French manager' by his critics, his methods were actually very British –

with a dash of continental autocracy added to the mix. Discipline, mental and physical fortitude, hard work and team camaraderie were all the tenets preached by Houllier. His was a pragmatic approach, building from the defence, and if his style of football was sometimes at odds with that craved by Kopites, this was tolerated when results went well. There can be little doubt that he brought a modernity to the club and did have a positive effect on players who would go on to become legends. For three years, Houllier was close to achieving iconic, nay messianic, status and he delivered three trophies in one remarkable campaign. Illness may have deprived him of some judgement and may have been partly responsible for his downfall and a revisionist outlook has changed many people's perception. The final two seasons were a mess but that should not take away from the phenomenal success that Houllier enjoyed prior to this.

His treatment of Robbie Fowler has also coloured his legacy and not in a favourable way. Paul Tomkins put it succinctly in *Dynasty*:

'The problem Houllier faced was that Fowler was 'untouchable' in the eyes of the fans, and that's always dangerous for the man who has to decide who plays. It seems pretty certain that Fowler was not an easy character to deal with, and one who made mistakes, but at the same time his account of Houllier's behaviour paints the picture of a man who couldn't cope with confrontation or deal with players on the straightest of levels.'

The Liverpool manager made the decision from a position of massive strength (and from his hospital bed) but the truth is that Fowler, in his subsequent career, never came close to regaining the spark of his earlier years. But football supporters tend to deal in currencies of what may have been (or what should have been, according to themselves). Some fans never forgave Houllier and once the rot set in, they were happy to give vent with their frustrations.

Gérard Houllier should be given the respect that is his due for some fine achievements. He may have lost his way as his tenure sometimes threatened to spiral into practical farce and he didn't win the Reds a league title, for which the fans were so desperate for. But then, these two charges are hardly unique in modern Liverpool management.

For a few months in the spring of 2001, Houllier got absolutely everything right and gave us some of our finest memories supporting the Reds. His subsequent failings should not let us forget this. It may have been that his illness was a direct contributing factor towards these failings; it may be only coincidence. But Liverpool, as a club, tend to be hard work for our managers, to inflict ageing and confusion as things unravel.

Houllier deserves more credit. He did, after all, very nearly pay the ultimate price.

CHAPTER 10 - OURS TO KEEP

Rafa Benítez's first season in English football will never be forgotten. It was the most miraculous of campaigns and the unlikeliest of stories. The surreal nature – the sheer insanity – of Liverpool's European escapades was given a semblance of reality, a dose of verisimilitude, by the Reds consistently struggling in the league. Rafa had to learn the unique idiosyncrasies of the English domestic game but he was already a master in the continental arena, having secured the UEFA Cup with Valencia.

It began with hope; not that we would etch our name on 'Oul Big Ears' again – that could not have been further from our minds – but hope that, after stagnation, things were moving in the right direction. The Spanish manager, usurper of the La Liga duopoly of Real Madrid and Barcelona, took over from a floundering Houllier, and Kopites greeted his appointment with huge optimism; we remembered his monolithic Valencia wiping the floor with us in recent seasons and we theoretically juxtaposed his achievements in Spain with what he could do to the heavy hitters of our league.

But before a ball was kicked, the Spaniard was under pressure. Our two English stars, Michael Owen and Steven Gerrard, were picturing greener pastures over the horizon. After some flirtation, Stevie eventually said no (or at least delayed a definitive rejection) to Russian millions and the wooing of a preening José Mourinho. Owen, however, with his contract running down, upped sticks to Real Madrid for a paltry £8.5 million, with Antonio Núñez arriving as a lightweight makeweight. He would not quicken Anfield pulses. Far more electric was the capture of Xabi Alonso (still this scribbler's favourite Liverpool player) from Real Sociedad for

£10.7 million. From the off, the midfielder showed himself to be an uber-controller of the tempo on a football field, a matador of the hurly burly with a divine touch and an even better brain. He was very much the general of Rafa's team and would go onto be part of possibly Liverpool's best ever modern midfield. Benítez also looked to his native country in signing Luis García and Josemi. The former would write himself into Red folklore with some stunning contributions to cup winning campaigns. Though he could frustrate, the little former Barcelona attacker had a heart (and a smile) as big as his diminutive frame and his name is still sung on the Kop. Josemi, after a decent start, faded rapidly.

A lot was expected from the other signing, a parting gift from Gérard Houllier. Djibril Cissé had been making waves in the French league for Auxerre (he had been recommended to Benítez while at Valencia and had apparently been told that securing the striker's acquisition would win him La Liga). Cissé would prove to be underwhelming but started the campaign very promisingly before a horrific leg break at Blackburn curtailed his inaugural English season. A player of immense physical gifts, the then record signing unfortunately could not marry his athleticism with brain waves.

Besides Michael Owen departing the ranks, there were three other stalwarts from the treble season departing. Markus Babbel could not recapture his form or fitness following his battle with illness and was moved on to VFB Stuttgart on a free. Danny Murphy, perhaps prematurely, was told by Benítez that they had accepted a £2.5 million offer from Charlton Athletic and he was free to go. Finally, a fading Stéphane Henchoz left for Celtic, also on a free transfer. It really did feel like a changing of the guard.

Early season struggles
'Stopping and then starting, taking off and landing' – Let Down, Radiohead.

It's fair to say that it took Rafa a while to get used to English football. The autumn months of the season – particularly domestically – were a depressing kaleidoscope of disappointment punctuated by moments when it looked like things may be about to click. Or at least that's the memory. In reality the results weren't that bad – at least not from a truly modern perspective – but it was the manner and pattern of defeats that irked. For example, in the space of five days the Reds suffered 1-0 reverses against the might of Grazer AK at Anfield (though the first leg had been a relatively comfortable 2-0 victory) and Bolton Wanderers. Then, following some encouraging displays, Liverpool endured a nightmare two weeks at the end of September: in the space of four games, the Reds suffered defeat to Manchester United, Olympiacos and Chelsea. By the time the Blues beat us at Stamford Bridge on 3rd October, Rafa's new team was in eleventh place, twelve points behind the league leaders, Arsenal. It looked like it was about to get worse too; the Reds went to Craven Cottage just after this bleak run of defeats and were 2-0 down by half time. But Liverpool gave an early indication of what would be the defining spirit of the campaign – refusal to lie down. They scored four times without reply in a thrilling second half, the introduction of Alonso serving as a catalyst as the maestro provided the impetus and nous to jolt Liverpool from their torpor. It was fitting that the Spaniard scored the game's best goal, a superb free kick to give the Reds a 79th minute lead.

Following this, Liverpool were then held to a frustrating 0-0 home draw in the Champions League against Deportivo La Coruña, meaning qualification for the knockout phase already looked dicey. A run of fixtures which typified the early season form then commenced: a routine 2-0 victory at home to Charlton, a 2-2 draw with Blackburn Rovers (the dark and dreary evening kick-off and the horrific injury to Cissé was indicative of how we all felt at this stage), Deportivo were then beaten in the Estadio Municipal De Riazor, breathing new life into our European campaign, before Birmingham City arrived at Anfield and defeated the Reds 1-0. A couple of weeks later, after it again looked like we may have turned a domestic corner when Milan Baroš managed to make his head down running style a virtue in scoring a hat-trick to defeat Crystal Palace, Middlesbrough exposed the fundamental deficiencies in the team by beating the Reds 2-0 at the Riverside. After thirteen games Liverpool were down to eighth in the table. Three days later, a Javier Saviola winner of dubious legality gave Monaco a 1-0 victory in France and left our dreams of qualification in tatters. It was late November and the season already looked like unravelling.

What a hit son!
'If you think I wink, I did Laugh politely at repeats' – One day like this, Elbow.

Two rockets that will live long in the memory from two very different players provided much of the narrative for the next part of the campaign. Neil Mellor's thirty yard volley has perhaps been airbrushed out of our memories by the momentous events that were about to unfold during this historic year. But it really was a strike worthy of toppling the champions. Mellor never quite cut it as a Liverpool player and was only in the team due to injury but he seized on some uncharacteristic hesitancy from the Gunners rearguard in the dying moments of the game and conjured an unlikely dipping shot that seemed to sail in slow motion past David Seaman. Pandemonium followed at Anfield.

But just nine days later even this bedlam on the terraces would be surpassed in a defining game, for Liverpool, for Rafa and for Steven Gerrard. The Reds needed to beat Olympiacos by two clear goals to qualify from their Champions League group. Midway through the first half, there was a sense of inevitability as bow-legged Rivaldo guided a low free kick through the wall and past a rooted Chris Kirkland. Liverpool now needed three goals to progress and as the players trudged off at the half time whistle, it looked an impossible task. After all, the Greeks were masters of the cynical foul, the contemptuous wasting of time. In short, this wasn't Fulham in the non-stop adrenaline fuelled discord of the Premier League. But Red hopes were revived when Sinama-Pongolle swept a low shot into the net early in the second half. Liverpool, willed on by a fervent crowd, surged forward but we watched with hearts in mouth as we looked increasingly susceptible to a devastating counter. With just over ten minutes left, Neil Mellor scored again. Anfield became a wall of sound and with time nearly up Steven Gerrard, from a Mellor knock down, hit a devastatingly beautiful arrow that nestled, amidst unbridled joy, into the far corner of the Greeks' net. This was destiny and inexorability and epoch-defining writ large; once the ball left the captain's foot we knew where it was going. And us with it. A moment gleaned from a comic book that still precipitates spines shivering. The papers the following morning mentioned 'Saint-Étienne' approximately four hundred times. It was that kind of night.

Despondency in the domestic cups
'Heaven knows I'm miserable now' – The Smiths.

After the intoxicating highs of the Olympiacos match, Liverpool returned to the relatively prosaic sphere of the Premier League. Results continued to be up and down and this would be the trend for the rest of the domestic campaign. In the League Cup, a mixture of kids and reserves had performed admirably and by January the Reds faced Watford in the semi-final. Benítez fielded a strong team for both ties and Liverpool dispatched The Hornets 2-0 on aggregate with Gerrard hitting both goals. Fernando Morientes, an aristocrat of the European striking arena, had arrived in what appeared a scoop. Alas, his lack of pace was a terminal problem for him in English football. He did, though, start the League Cup Final against Chelsea, the Premier League champions elect. Mourinho's upstarts had destroyed all before them and were a mammoth twenty five points ahead of Liverpool in the league as the teams lined up in the Millennium Stadium. John Arne Riise looked to have won the game with another howitzer but there was a sting in the tail. Gerrard, heartbreakingly, headed into his own goal with minutes remaining, giving the Portuguese attention-grabber all the opportunity he needed to mock Kopites throughout the stadium. In extra time, the Blues ran out 3-2 winners. But if revenge is a dish best served cold, we only had to wait until it was lukewarm to inflict our reprisal with relish.

A few weeks before this, what we then thought of as our only other realistic hope of silverware had ended in tragi-comic circumstances. Rafa – in a classic damned if you do, damned if you don't scenario – just three days after Manchester United had beaten us at Anfield, sent out some of the reserves in the FA Cup at Burnley. The likes of Zak Whitbread, David Raven, Darren Potter and John Welsh all featured as a laughably inept attempt at a Cruyff turn from Djimi Traoré resulted in a farcical own goal and a 1-0 victory to the Clarets. Benítez now found himself under pressure as four days later Southampton defeated the Reds 2-0 in the league. Three defeats in a row – the manager doesn't get English football, it's a disgrace to rotate against lower league opposition: the die of criticism that the Spaniard would face in England had been cast. But, ultimately, salvation and redemption awaited in Europe.

Continental Escapades
'Bound by wild desire, I fell into a ring of fire' – *Ring of Fire, Johnny Cash.*

The Reds had been handed what appeared to be a tricky last sixteen tie against Bayer Leverkusen, but after thirty five minutes of the home leg, Liverpool were 2-0 ahead courtesy of an adroit finish by García and a free kick from Riise that, unusually for him, actually went in (the Norwegian gloried in the Roberto Carlos syndrome because of that screamer against United in the 01/02 season). By the time another free kick from Hamann made it 3-0, it was looking like plain sailing. However, a mistake from Dudek in the last minute allowed França to give the Germans hope for the return leg. Nothing, it would appear, would be easy this season and there was no little trepidation as we arrived in the BayArena, four days after Newcastle had inflicted another league defeat. That França away goal made things look ropey but Luis García had other ideas and had fired the Reds to a 5-1 aggregate lead by the thirty second minute. Baroš added another and we were through to an unlikely quarter-final against the giants of Turin, Juventus.

With the curious providence that football often throws up, the first meeting of the two sides since Heysel was also the twentieth anniversary of the tragedy. On an emotional night in Anfield, Luis García, rapidly crystallising into a cult hero in the European arena, added to Sami Hyypiä's cultured opener with a dipping volley that any player in our illustrious history would have been proud of. Gianluigi Buffon was left clutching thin air as the ball fairly flew into the net to the delight and incredulity of a heaving Kop. It felt like a joyous throwback; a picture that had been painted in the seventies and eighties being dusted off and again put on display for a delirious crowd. Liverpool coped well with Juventus' vaunted attack until the sixty third minute when young Scott Carson – recently signed from Leeds United – allowed a routine Fabio Cannavaro header to slip inside his near post. A vital away goal and one that changed the complexion of the tie; the Italians were now favourites to progress.

In Turin, the Reds put on a tactical masterclass, again reminiscent of the halcyon days when we ruled Europe. Though there was many a nervy moment, Liverpool's goal was rarely troubled. Improbably, deliciously, we were in the Champions League Semi-Final where the runaway league leaders in England, José's Machiavellian mercenaries, awaited.

The first game at Stamford Bridge gave graphic notice of the rapidity with which Rafa was learning. Though Chelsea, in what would become typical of their manager's style, did not show huge ambition, the Reds stifled the game and may even have nicked it when a couple of chances fell their way. Frank Lampard though, effortless scorer of vital goals all season, missed the game's best chance. A 0-0 draw appeared to have both camps relatively optimistic about the return. Anfield was primed for a night that will long live in the memory.

We all know what happened in the next extraordinary game, in a cacophonous cauldron of passion and aching desire; it's imprinted onto our very consciousness but Jamie Carragher, in his autobiography, summed it up:

'Nothing I had experienced compared to the evening of May 3, 2005. Even during the warming up the volume of noise was several decibels higher than most league games. The Kop was full early, there were more banners and scarves than I could remember, and a full repertoire of songs escorted us through our preparations … Chelsea players were affected by the surge of absolute conviction coming from the stands. They'd later admit they had never known an atmosphere like it.'

Didi Hamann, another hero of the campaign, also described the magic in the air:

'Just every so often you sense a feeling in and around a football ground that is different from the normal experience," wrote Hamann. "Even as we arrived at the ground there seemed to be something special in the air that night and there was a special feeling about the place. As we prepared to come on to the pitch it seemed the rafters were shaking, such was the intensity of the crowd. They sang relentlessly and as we emerged from the tunnel, we were hit by a wave of noise, which was to continue for the whole night. We were one up early on and the noise from the crowd, that earlier had seemed like it couldn't get any louder, just got louder.'

An early goal in this type of game is never good for the nerves; we knew that all Chelsea needed was one to knock us out and make García's 'ghost goal' essentially irrelevant. Simultaneously, there was an air of defiance and almost an expectation that the hated Blues would inevitably score and who will forget Eiður Guðjohnsen's shot at the death that flew across the goal and narrowly wide.

Carragher again:

The Ring of Fire chants set the Kop ablaze during the final stressful seconds, as supporters maniacally waved their scarves above their heads, pleading for the final whistle.'

When the final whistle did come, it was genuinely extraordinary. It wasn't just an echo of the glory days; it was something enchanting and surreal. A squad of players containing the likes of Traoré, Biščan, Warnock, Mellor, Núñez and Baroš had made it to the European Champions League final.

Mourinho – like Rafa in his debut season in England, but the polar opposite in character – and one whom had danced a merry jig through the Premier League, was left to sulk and splutter. Benítez had defeated him tactically and this was the start of a fierce rivalry between the pair.

The greatest European Cup Final of all time

'Walk on, walk on, with hope in your heart' – You'll never walk alone
Liverpool fans, half time at the Atatürk Stadium.

There've been a few words written on this final before, you know. Just a few. No words of mine can compare and let's be clear, no musings of any writer – no matter the talent – can do that night justice.

The greatest night of my life supporting Liverpool. No, screw that, probably the greatest night of my life full stop.

There are images in my head of the game; it's not really a narrative, more a collection of sequences, a dream-like, foggy but, at the same time, gloriously bright collection of pictures and scenes. It's a miraculously beautiful visage hewn from obstinate granite, it's the gift of fire from Prometheus, the spark of life handed to Adam in the Sistine Chapel. It's a child's first laugh, the sound of beauty and innocence; it's a lover's smile in the morning sun, the warmth of the knowledge that everything is okay; it's the feeling of a soul soaring to hitherto unattainable heights, the joyous all enveloping feeling of freedom.

It was also a fucking roller coaster of epic proportions.

Images, just images is all I can supply.

Maldini, the Roman god, scores early. We refuse to let our heads go down in the face of the worst possible start. Nesta might have given away a penalty. There are more Milan chances as we hang on. Kaká, probably the best player on the planet, is tormenting the Liverpool defence like some prodigious ten year old playing *FIFA* against his father. Through-ball after through-ball; Carragher flailing, Dudek floundering. 3-0 Milan and the feeling is way beyond despair. It's horror and dismay but more, it's a dread anticipation that there is additional misery to come, that we are to be truly embarrassed, that all of our hopes and dreams are about to be dashed cruelly upon the altar of a magnificently gifted football team, perhaps the best in Europe. Rival English fans are gloating already. 'Haha, the scousers and their expectations, their sense of dubious entitlement'.

You will never walk alone.

It's half-time and the crowd, all flag waving and refusal to give up, do their club proud.

Eerily, quietly at first and then gathering volume until it's an eardrum-splitting decibel of passion and fervour. You will never walk alone. Whatever happens now, lads, we're proud of this team and of our club.

Gerrard. That man again. Impossible header, looping over Dida. Watch his body move again, watch every tendon of his wired body strain to generate the force required. Then watch him cajole and entreat the crowd. 'Come fucking on, give us your all, we will give you our sweat, our blood but give us your voice.'

The crowd respond, the noise goes through the roof. Milan players look at each other. This does not happen; these mad lads don't know they're beaten.

Šmicer fires in number two. Eruptions and embracing. We're back in it. We're right back fucking in it. Milan can sense it too; they can sense the grim reaper of fate, the inexorable force of gravity, the unfolding poetry we're privileged to witness. Suddenly it seems inevitable. Gerrard, smelling the panic like a rabid bloodhound, races onto a Baroš through-ball. Penalty.

Alonso, already a hero, steps up looking like he would – suddenly – prefer to be anywhere else. He can feel the relentless press of history. Because this is historic. Dida guesses correctly and palms the ball away. For one horrible moment we feel a deflation that is like a knife to the stomach. But then ecstasy, pure and unadulterated, as Xabi follows up and crashes the rebound into the roof of the net.

Three goals in five bonkers minutes.

Extra time is still an aeon away. The heroic effort has taken everything from these players. Gerrard has to move to right-back; his performance from then on is nothing short of superhuman. As is Carragher's; it feels, looking back, that he is perpetually throwing his fatigued body in the way of a shot, constantly clearing, consistently shouting and organising, sinews taut and limbs stretched to breaking point. His face is haggard from exhaustion, furrowed in concentration, in defiance. Traore clears a goal-bound effort off the line. They are all heroes on that pitch, every one of them.

Extra time. More nerves that make the Chelsea experience in Anfield feel like the optimistic anticipation of a new season. Andriy Shevchenko, deadly and ruthless, receives the ball three yards out with the goal gaping. This is it. It's gone now, snatched away after we'd been given new hope.

Except Dudek somehow saves the initial shot and then, like a cocaine-addled Superman, flings a hand above and unbelievably keeps out the follow-up.

'Name on the cup,' exclaims Andy Gray sagely.

And who are we to argue as penalties begin.

As soon as Serginho misses the first kick, the Milan players know. There may be a lot more penalties to come, but they know. This has been written for a while now. It's Liverpool's trophy, it has always been Liverpool's trophy. From the very beginning, back in August as a fresh-faced Spaniard took his place in the dugout.

Shevchenko again, the weight of the Reds' destiny perched on his shoulders. He has to score or Liverpool will become champions of Europe for the fifth time. Dudek, after Carragher's gentle coaxing, recalls the spirit of Rome in 1984 and dances on the goal line. The camera is behind the Ukrainian striker who two years previously had won the cup for Milan in similar circumstances. But this time the inexorable and merciless sense of Liverpool fate cannot be brokered with; we know he is going to miss as he shoots tamely at the Reds' Polish 'keeper. We have just long enough to see the ball rebounding to Shevchenko as he volleys it in a superfluous gesture of frustration before the camera pans to the Liverpool players who take off in a jubilant mass of arms and grins.

Liverpool Football Club are champions of Europe.

The love affair with Rafa had begun. In a season of domestic underachievement (the Reds finished fifth in the Premier League with Everton claiming the last Champions League place – not that it made any difference in the long term), Liverpool's and Benítez's redemption came in Europe. But, of course, it was more than mere redemption; it was a triumph of almost miraculous intent. From Stevie's third against Olympiacos to Hyypiä's lethal finish against Juventus, from García's Terry Mac impression in the same game to Guðjohnsen's miss, from 3-0 down against a miserly defence in Istanbul to the most astonishing comeback of all time. It was simply epic, the whole incredible, wonderful journey.

It was Liverpool. The only club in the world that this type of thing can happen to.

CHAPTER 11 - HER SAD CAPTAIN

In her dreams, he never slips. The grotesque twist of fate never takes place, none of it takes place. Her mind has ejected the entire game from her memories; there is no pass from Mamadou Sakho, there is no Demba Ba, the countless attempts at atonement from Stevie don't occur, there is no tragic denouement as a former Red breaks clear for Chelsea.

She has, almost subliminally, airbrushed those ninety minutes from her brain. The build-up remains, the parade of red and white, the heaving throngs bedecked in Liverpool's colours, the coach arriving, carrying the heroes to their date with destiny, to the Premier League title.

The final memory she allows herself is of Stevie as he waits in the tunnel. She savours his eyes set in concentration; she knows the formidable intelligence and the brooding intensity that lurk behind those crinkly eyes.

Then there is a mental blink, a slip in her consciousness, and as she lies in the early morning sun, as a stream of light meanders through her blinds and into her apartment, she mouths the words, paraphrasing as a tear slowly rolls down her cheeks:

"Another sunrise with my sad captain."

The song 'My Sad Captains', from Elbow's album *The Take-off and Landing of Everything*, is a constant soundtrack to this grief. It is the day after Crystal Palace and every fibre of her being screams at the injustice of it all.

"Another sunrise with my sad captain."

Steven Gerrard – her captain – will not get a Premier League title. Not now. Fate has again conspired against the Reds. The cruelty of it is rending, a slashing knife, a scythe from a robed spectre. It has consumed her every waking thought.

There is another mental blink and suddenly she is transported to a pub in the city centre. She is sitting with her father – a season ticket holder and the person most responsible for her obsession – and his brother. The pub is packed with supporters who could not make the trip to Newcastle this soon after Christmas, jubilant at another convincing win for Rafa's Reds. She is nineteen years of age and enjoying the warmth of a pint and the delicious feeling that Liverpool are top of the league.

Her father turns to her uncle, while simultaneously gathering her by her shoulder, welcoming her into the fold. He knocks back approximately half of his pint, his Adam's apple bobbing furiously, and then exclaims:

'I'm fucking well telling yous, Gerrard's the best in the world at the moment. You can take your Ronaldinhos or your Rooneys … Stevie's better than the lot. That was the best I've seen from a Liverpool player since Kenny in his pomp.'

She nods in silent acquiescence, her pride at hearing these words from the one man that can rival Stevie in her affections, robbing her of her speech. Instead she mentally probes the highlights of the game for the umpteenth time since the final whistle as she raises a glass to her lips.

Lucas' through ball to an onrushing Stevie, who has timed his run to perfection behind the Magpies' defence, is sublime. Shay Given, beleaguered and having performed heroics thus far to keep the goals to three, comes out to try to narrow the angle. Gerrard's control of the ball is perfect, immaculate, and with contemptuous ease he flicks the ball over the Newcastle goalkeeper and into the empty net. Her heart is bursting as she flails about, along with the rest of the Liverpool fans that she is surrounded by. The captain has led the Reds back to the top of the league….

With an almost physical wrench she is back in the present, back in the reality where the Reds have let that title slip away again. She rises from her bed and pads towards the window where she opens the blinds and lights a cigarette. She picks up her mobile and scrolls to that song. The song that seems to warble to her soul, the melancholy of which is matched only by the torment that she cannot shake. She hits play and, looking out over the city as it begins to wake, saviours the strangely satisfying ache of loss.

"I'm running out of miracles," comes the haunting vocals from the speakers.

"My sad captain," she says to herself again and exhales smoke slowly.

That curious blink occurs again, that doubling within her brain, and she is in Anfield. The pitch is gloriously lit up by the floodlights, a wondrous tapestry upon which anything can be painted. The night is freezing and she pulls her coat around her while tightening her red scarf. The crowd around her is a sea, a seething mass of defiance, an ocean of refusal to give in. One more goal. Just one more goal. She is screaming, a lung busting cacophonous tirade of entreaty to her team.

Jamie Carragher crosses the ball from deep, towards Neil Mellor. The striker does well in cushioning a header towards the Liverpool skipper as he sprints towards it.

What happens then, she will never forget. Ever, as long as she draws breath.

As the ball was lashed by Stevie towards the Olympiakos goal, as it soared with inexorable trajectory towards the net, so something soared within her. From her belly, through her chest and up through her throat, finally to be given some semblance of relief as it gushed from her mouth; a tribal wail of triumph, a roar of ecstasy.

As Stevie ran towards the crowd, as the hysterics threatened to overwhelm her, something awoke within her. A primal, ruthless and grasping force, a force that a fifteen year old girl would forever associate with Stevie.

Back in the present, she flicks the cigarette out of the window and turns to head towards the shower. She stops with a jolt, as a sigh barely escapes her mouth, as her hands move to her face in an instinctive display of shock.

Stevie is sitting on her bed.

He is wearing the suit he wore before the Chelsea game. It looks slightly unkempt; the tie loosened, a hint of white from the shirt which is cascading from under the blazer. He smiles that self-deprecating smile and says:

"Enough with the song, love."

She is aware that he is not really here. On some level she is aware of that fact. Her tired mind has summoned him, like a djinn from a bottle, to bestow a wish or a great boon upon her.

Abstractly she wonders has she, in fact, gone insane. But she mentally shrugs and decides to go along with this turn of events; it is her subconscious sitting on that sheet-strewn bed, she fancies. Before she can really think about this further, she asks the Stevie apparition the first thing that enters her head.

"Aren't you sad?"

He grins, the eyes crinkle, and he gazes away from her almost sheepishly.

"I am a bit," he starts. He appears stuck for words and seems to be considering what to say. Finally he looks at her and adds:

"But it's okay, that's just the way things go. Poetry doesn't always rhyme; sometimes it just hurts."

She nods and thinks to herself that she worships this footballer; always has and always will. The week before, in a frenzy of torment, she had posted something on her blog as she tried to define what it was that Stevie meant to her and to millions of Liverpool supporters all over the world. She gazes at her captain and recalls the words:

There have been players who could shoot better than Steven Gerrard. There have been better headers of a ball, better dribblers, and more effective tacklers. There have been players who were faster sprinters and who could run for longer, footballers who could ping a more effective cross or launch a better long pass. There have been players who had more impressive vision, who saw an unlikely pass three or four steps before anyone else, and had the technical ability to execute it.

But there has probably never been a player who could combine all of these facets to such a high degree as Steven Gerrard. Make no mistake, if you are reading these words you are privileged as your life coincided with the career of a once-in-a-generation footballer. A scouser who rose through the ranks, a dyed in the red Liverpudlian who went on to captain his club to Champions League success, a young man who had stood starry-eyed on the Kop and became one of the greatest players to ever wear the Liver Bird upon his chest.

We love our gods to have feet of clay and the Steven Gerrard legend is tainted; flirtation with Chelsea and the part he played in the downfall of a manager caused many to lose some love for the midfielder. He was a hero with flaws and he played a central role in his own footballing tragedy on the pitch; a giant of the modern game whose own piece of poor control spelled the end of his title dream; a fiendishly cruel twist of fate that cast a pall over an entire football club.

He'd been melting for years and, save for a brief and glorious rebirth as a holding midfielder this season, his powers had long been on the wane. We witnessed all of this; we witnessed a force of nature becoming an average Joe. We viewed this complex character as he struggled with his own footballing mortality, as his dark pride was ravaged by years, as his brooding cleverness came to terms with the march of time.

But, right now, let us remind ourselves that one of the greatest players to ever play for our beloved club gave us so many memories. The Premier League era has thrown up some fine footballers for many different sides. But Steven Gerrard, a footballer hewn in the image of Roy Race, moulded from the dreams of every supporter that ever stood on a terrace, will never be equalled or repeated.

A one-off, a footballer that belongs in the ranks of footballing deities, up there with Billy Liddell and Kenny Dalglish. Remind yourself that you witnessed it. Let the supporters of rival clubs sing about him slipping, let them glory in the fact that that league title will more than likely remain tantalisingly elusive. We have the legend.

"I thought the blog would ease the pain, Stevie," she says to him. "I thought it could banish that fucking game, that fucking slip. It's beyond cruel. How could it happen?"

He just looks at her and nods.

"Believe me, I struggled. I really struggled. But remember Fulham?"

There is another blink, the curious doubling is back and her bedroom fades from her vision. Replacing it is Craven Cottage on a Wednesday night with the Reds 1-0 down. She is with the other away fans; it's only a few days since Arsenal were obliterated and how typical, how Liverpool, would defeat here be. The apprehension and tension is palpable all around her; frustration bites wickedly as another attack breaks down when suddenly, almost from nowhere, as if plucked from the sheer power of his formidable will, Stevie stops the Fulham counter attack dead and launches a bewilderingly precise pass. The ball is struck with the outside of his foot as the captain is falling and it is a gorgeous, dissecting ball to Sturridge. In her heart of hearts, she knows that Stevie's powers are on the wane but there are only a couple of players in the entire league that could play this ball. 1-1 and game on. 1-1 and dreams are still alive; a winner is infinitely possible with the entirety of the second half still to come.

Except, of course, it is never that easy – has never, ever been that easy in all the time that Stevie has been in the side. Routine victories, a 2-0 for example, are always few and far between. With the game inching towards full-time, with the clock counting with agonising rapidity and now entering the eighty-ninth minute, Liverpool win a penalty. Up he steps, up steps Steven Gerrard, with the weight of all away supporters within Craven Cottage on his shoulders, with tangible tension suffocating her and all around her.

He buries the spot kick, hammers it home, and it is his celebration – as he whirls in triumph and rips off his red shirt – that gives birth to her own belief. The captain believes that this is no longer about securing top four; this about a title charge. The belief courses through her veins and the elation and relief and pride and jubilation surge through her; it is intoxicating and heady, a wine that has taken years to ferment.

"That's when I believed, Stevie," she sniffs. "That's when I thought we could do it. But it hurts even thinking back to it. It's what Dante wrote in 'Inferno': 'there is no greater woe than in misery to remember the happy time'-"

She is interrupted.

"But you did believe. You had that elation and so did I. It lasted for nearly three months, it propelled a magical ride."

He pauses again and shakes his head.

"Here's the thing. There's been a final named after me, there've been hat-tricks against Everton, there's been two Champions League finals, there's been the treble year, there've been too many long shots to count, too many times the ball just flew into the net. There was scoring that goal against United, announcing myself to you fully as Barthez perfunctorily dived. There was Torres and me, a dance of telepathy that weaved its way around a continent, as we defied the odds over and over. I grew up standing near where you stand every week and I captained my club to too many great days and nights to remember. The pain of near misses accentuates the glory and the splendour makes the grief easier to live with. For every slip, every mistake, there was a thing of wonder. And always, like a shining beacon, above all the memories, there was the fact that I could call myself a king of Europe.

There was Istanbul, a night no Red will ever forget, a night football will never forget, and if my penance, if the trade off, was that I am destined never to get that league title, well, that's okay. I'm the captain of Liverpool Football Club, where success and failure are always intertwined. For many I was Liverpool Football Club. I have known dizzying success, attainment and achievement tasted by very few. I have made mistakes, I have flirted with enemies, I have failed at times. I have been human, not the superman you think of me. I am a fragile being but something, some force, marked me out for great things. The ballet of success and failure, the embroidery of apposition that is my club, was manifested by me. Yes, I am sad but I am also eternally grateful; the two can exist side by side. We should celebrate the glory of Icarus trying to reach the sun, rather than mourning his fall."

She knows this is taking place in her head and closes her eyes with gratitude. Her captain – her sad captain – has shown that he is anything but. Her subconscious has reminded her that, in supporting Liverpool, we have to embrace the bittersweet; it is our legacy and our DNA. She walks to the shower, a fragrant ache having replaced the grim hollowness of loss in her chest.

Outside, as she makes her way to work she is surrounded by the remnants of revelry from the night before. There is the rustling of empty crisp packets, caught in a slight breeze, as she walks towards the railway station and they seem to whisper to her, even to sing, and it is an ode of promise, of triumph juxtaposed with tragedy, of loss and victory, of love and heartache. It whispers of Istanbul and of forty yard equalisers in the dying embers of a cup final. It sings of her sad captain, of kissing a camera at Old Trafford (more than once) and of pride in wearing the Liver Bird on his chest.

Countless goals, countless cajoling, countless tackles and long balls and fighting. Over and over, she hears that word, almost sibilant, at once coming from near and far, and she knows that she has been blessed.

Istanbul.

Istanbul.

She has lived through the greatest miracle of modern football and she has been a fan through a time when her club possessed one of its greatest ever servants.

She walks into the station, blinking away tears that have shed some of their bitterness.

She is proud to be a Liverpool fan and is proud of her captain, now no longer merely sad but also triumphant, a symbol of the city and of the club.

CHAPTER 12 - CONSOLIDATION AND CUP FINALS

How does one top arguably the greatest night in the history of the club? The answer was twofold for many Liverpool fans: keep Steven Gerrard and mount another genuine title challenge. The former would be ultimately successful; although it looked for a spell as if it would end with the captain jumping ship to Chelsea, Gerrard's genuine love for the club overcame his demons of self-doubt. The latter – attempting to wrest the Premier League from London and Manchester United – would be infinitely more challenging and it would take a few years of tweaking and consolidation before a genuine title tilt would become a reality.

Rafa Benítez knew the faults in his squad: comprehensive defeats at the likes of Bolton, Birmingham City and Southampton in the 04/05 campaign had convinced the Liverpool manager that pace, power, consistency of performance and a genuine target man were prerequisites to succeed in the physically demanding English Premier League. Pepe Reina arrived for the sometimes slipshod Dudek who, fresh from his Istanbul heroics, would have to make do as a reserve before he departed to warm the bench in Madrid. A month after resurrecting the ghost of Bruce Grobbelaar in Rome, the Pole's career as a first choice elite goalkeeper was effectively over. Indeed, the miraculous complexion of the Champions League Final and the improbable nature of the feat were graphically displayed with the fact that three stalwarts of that campaign, Baroš, Šmicer and Biščan, also departed, while Hamann and Traoré would now only play a bit-part role. Peter Crouch – after terrorising Liverpool's rearguard for Southampton the previous January – arrived for £7 million. The striker was seen as the clichéd 'big man with a good touch', who could keep the ball in opposition danger zones and bring others into play; a role he performed laudably well in his time with the Reds. Mohamed Sissoko was signed from Valencia, under the noses of Everton, to add some steel and nous. Sometimes looking like a world beater, the Malian ultimately lacked the technical ability to really make an impact (although injury would also play a part in his Anfield career not being what Rafa hoped it would be). Finally, in January, the Liverpool manager added Daniel Agger, a stylish Danish centre-back, to the ranks and, to the delight of Liverpool fans everywhere, reunited them with one of their favourite sons. Robbie Fowler was back in a Liverpool shirt.

The 05/06 season was a curious one that started in mid-July, thanks to UEFA caught out by the unlikely event of a Champions League winner finishing outside the top four. The Welsh part timers TNS ("they'll be dancing on the streets of Total Network Solutions tonight"!) and the Lithuanian side, FBK Kaunas, were expectedly and comprehensively dispatched before autumn set in; the Reds finally took their place in the group stages of Europe's flagship competition with a 3-2 aggregate win over CSKA Sofia that included a 1-0 home defeat. Rafa's problems with trying to build and juggle his squad were evidently far from over.

This emphatically proved the case as Liverpool's poor domestic form continued from the 04/05 season. Draws were undermining the Reds' start to the campaign and by the time Fulham systematically dispatched Liverpool in late October, Rafa was staring grimly at another massively underwhelming league season. With Liverpool languishing in twelfth place, already a frankly ridiculous seventeen points behind the defending champions, Chelsea, the Liverpool manager would probably have come under some close scrutiny by Kopites if a fifth European title had not been secured so memorably.

But Benítez was building and it would not be long before we began to see the fruits of his labour: the following nine league games in a row were won (while only conceding one goal – a truly phenomenal achievement), resulting in the Reds lying in third spot by the turn of the year. It was a position they held onto and some stunning form in the last few months of the campaign resulted in a superb finishing points haul of eighty two; a twenty four point improvement on the previous season. Moreover, the Reds won all nine of their league games from the 15th March until the end of the season. Clearly, Rafa was coming to terms with the unique eccentricities of English football.

Punctuating this remarkable run had been the World Club Championship which Liverpool, for all their previous success, had never won before. Rafa badly wanted this trophy to add to 'oul Big Ears' but after a 3-0 semi-final win over Deportivo Saprissa in Japan's Yokohama International Stadium, the Reds were defeated 1-0 by São Paulo in the final of an event that perhaps the club itself valued more for the marketing potential than for any serious worth. Nevertheless, the Liverpool manager showed his commitment to the Reds (and, it has to be said, his icy detachment) by staying in the Orient with the team after receiving news that his father had died.

The defence of the Champions League had seen the Reds – with that curious diabolical serendipity that football rejoices in throwing up – drawn with Chelsea in their group. The rivalry between Benítez and Mourinho was by now entering a cloud of toxicity, not least thanks to the poisonous barbs flung routinely by the Portuguese, who was now seeing his Spanish rival as a genuine threat. Home and away scoreless draws with the Blues and routine victories over Real Betis and Anderlecht saw the Reds top their group. Alas, in the first knockout round against Benfica, Liverpool succumbed to a 3-0 aggregate defeat; failed transfer target Simão Sabrosa predictably scoring the killer first away goal for the Portuguese champions.

Europe may have been uncharacteristically sparse terrain for Benítez, but there were more than a few crumbs of comfort in what was a thrilling FA Cup campaign. The scene was set at an icily cold Kenilworth Road in early January as the Reds came back from 3-1 down to beat Luton Town to win 5-3 with Xabi Alonso repeating his Newcastle trick from a few months previous and scoring from his own half. But it was two ties against the domestic heavyweights Manchester United and Chelsea that really caught the imagination of Reds' fans and gave us real hope that we could win the trophy. A superbly finished Peter Crouch goal gave Liverpool the spoils at Anfield against Ferguson's charges and then, for the second season in a row, Benítez outwitted José Mourinho in the semi-final of a competition as Riise and García secured a 2-1 victory. Just for good measure, the Reds also crushed Birmingham City 7-0, the highest win of Rafa's reign thus far.

Once more, the Millennium Stadium beckoned and a Saturday afternoon showdown with Alan Pardew's West Ham. To call it a topsy-turvy game would be doing the emotions most Reds were subjected to a gross disservice, and the Hammers raced into a 2-0 lead against a strangely reticent Liverpool. Steven Gerrard, casting off the last lingering gremlins of self-doubt and now ready to fully embrace his role as his club's saviour, then contributed a dazzling assist for Cissé before half-time, and his own adept finish brought the Reds level. But it looked as if his heroics would be in vain as Paul Konchesky (not for the last time) threatened to break Liverpool hearts with a cross that somehow found Reina's top corner. Reds fans looked on in disbelief as their team huffed and puffed in the stifling heat and there was a sense of resignation as the clock ticked past the ninetieth minute; surely another comeback – almost exactly a year after the mother of all comebacks – was not on the cards?

But what happened next, no Liverpool fan will forget. The strike from Gerrard has become part of the very fabric of the legend of the club and cemented his iconic status. In his recent autobiography, the Liverpool captain put words to the almost surreal train of events that occurred:

'... *Danny Gabbidon won the challenge and headed clear. The ball bounced a long way from goal, once, then twice. Almost magnetically, the ball arced towards me. I was thirty-five yards away. I was too tired to take possession and set off on a surging run towards goal. Instinctively, I decided to hit it first time. I caught it on the rise, dregs of energy rippling down from my clenched right leg and my crashing boot into the flight of the ball.*

I caught it like a dream. I followed its searing blur. I hit it so perfectly it was hard to track it in the air. My shot flew and flew. A few seconds stretched and then ... bang!

The West Ham net billowed and shook in shock. I had to look again. Had I really just done that? Goal!'

Following the thunderbolt from Liverpool's captain, it was Pepe Reina's turn to fortify himself in Reds' affections with a near miraculous save from Nigel Reo-Coker before performing heroics during the penalty shoot-out as the Spaniard saved three of the Hammers' efforts.

Summer optimism was rampant as Gerrard lifted the FA Cup; a World Cup was in the post and Kopites looked forward to the next season with huge buoyancy. Following the thrilling cup success and the nature of the fantastic end to the league season, Liverpool fans were tentatively anticipating a genuine title challenge for the following campaign.

But if the hope kills you, anticipation surely slaughters you. Even since the last genuine tilt at the Premier League, the goal posts had, again, shifted considerably. Chelsea, bankrolled by the billions of Abramovich and coached by the pragmatic excellence of Mourinho, had posted ninety plus point finishes in 04/05 and 05/06. Manchester United were fast emerging from their relative transition and could now boast a formidable strike force that included a rapidly maturing Rooney and Ronaldo. In short – and contrary to previous seasons where the Reds had won the league – there would now be little margin for error.

In the previous close season, Benítez had successfully identified exactly how his team would improve and bought accordingly. Now, looking to add goals, the Liverpool manager had to be more surgical. Craig Bellamy and Dirk Kuyt were brought in from Blackburn Rovers and Feyenoord respectively to bolster Liverpool's striking options. The former, a pacey Welsh firebrand, capable of looking world class and mundane from game to game, was an undoubted risk that never really worked out. The latter would achieve huge respect from the Kop, if never quite iconic status; Kuyt was brought in as a prolific goal scorer but soon metamorphosed into a hard working attacker, usually from the right flank, who still contributed with many a vital goal. More puzzling was the signing of Jermaine Pennant from Birmingham City for a fee of £6.7 million. Presumably bought to supply bullets for Crouch (whose heading – though good – was weaker than one would imagine given his height), Pennant was only capable of playing as a right winger and, though he had some good moments with Liverpool, ultimately flattered to deceive. Much more successful was the monster defensive midfielder Javier Mascherano, inexplicably languishing in the West Ham reserves, whom Benítez brought in following a debilitating eye injury to Sissoko. Finally, the Latino full-back pair of Álvaro Arbeloa and Fábio Aurélio arrived, the latter in the January transfer window.

There were few highlights in the early season and emblematic of the inconsistent form was the qualification round for the Champions League where Liverpool were perhaps fortunate to overcome Maccabi Haifa 3-2 on aggregate. In the first leg at Anfield, the Reds were drawing 1-1 with a couple of minutes to go before Mark González, who was making his debut, eventually scored to settle nerves to a degree. The return leg had to be played in Kiev due to political upheaval in Israel, and the Reds looked painfully rusty with a Peter Crouch goal in the second half securing a nervy draw. 'Europe may not be quaking, but the 2005 winners can breathe a huge sigh of relief,' wrote *The Guardian* in what turned out to be a less than prescient prediction.

There were also initial domestic travails for Liverpool as some damaging results – including a 3-0 reverse against Everton at Goodison Park – threatened to derail the season before it really got going. The now annual league defeats by Chelsea and Manchester United followed, and though the Reds form picked up as the season progressed, by the time Paul Scholes and Rio Ferdinand handed Liverpool's rivals a 2-0 win at Old Trafford in late October, Liverpool were languishing in eleventh. There was little panic however, from the majority of Liverpool's support; failure to finish in the top four was not really a huge concern although the first nascent whisperings of doubt in Benítez 's tenure from some of the fan base started around this time. The Reds' interest in both domestic cups ended in January within three days of each other as Arsenal twice defeated Liverpool by an aggregate score of 9-4. But, typically under Rafa, league form improved; Liverpool were always capable of putting three or four wins together to enable them to climb the table and, following a brilliant 4-1 dismantling of Arsenal on the last day of March, in which Crouch scored the perfect hat-trick of a header and shot with either foot, the Reds were sitting comfortably in fourth, five points ahead of their nearest rivals and with a game in hand. Two defeats away to Portsmouth and Fulham in the last few weeks of the season could be explained by European commitments and Liverpool would eventually finish third on sixty eight points, ahead of Arsenal on goal difference, but a massive twenty one points behind the new champions Manchester United.

However, these continental commitments were bearing hugely

pleasing fruits. The Reds negotiated a group containing PSV Eindhoven, Galatasaray and Bordeaux with ease but the Catalan footballing aristocracy of Barcelona, favourites for the competition, awaited Liverpool in the first knockout stage. They may not have reached the point of their evolutionary path that would see them hailed as one of the greatest club sides of all time, but Barcelona could still call on the formidable and daunting talents of Ronaldinho, Gianluca Zambrotta, Xavi, Carles Puyol, Andrés Iniesta and a Lionel Messi just beginning to establish himself as the best player in the world. A week before the first leg in the Camp Nou, John Arne Riise and Craig Bellamy had been involved in a late night ruckus during an Algarve break; this may have sealed Bellamy's eventual departure from Liverpool, but it was strangely and perversely apt that it was these two who scored the goals in a famous 2-1 victory. In particular, the Welsh striker's 'golf swing' celebration as he netted a 74th minute winner will live long in the memory. The Reds managed to advance to the quarter-finals on away goals although Eiður Guðjohnsen, who two years previously had nearly broke Liverpool's hearts when playing for Chelsea, ensured a nervy final fifteen minutes at Anfield.

Liverpool's reward for knocking out Barcelona was a reuniting tie with PSV Eindhoven, who themselves had eliminated Arsenal. The first leg in Holland saw Rafa's Liverpool at their ruthless, efficient best and goals from Gerrard, Crouch and Riise handed the Reds an emphatic 3-0 victory. Ronald Koeman brought his charges to Anfield a week later and looked on as Liverpool gave a controlled and measured performance with Crouch again getting on the scoresheet. Another date with destiny beckoned as the Reds would now meet Chelsea for a place in Athens against either Manchester United or AC Milan.

The Londoners may have been about to relinquish their Premier League title, but José Mourinho was determined – and probably expectant – to achieve European success. Chelsea had only suffered defeat once so far in the Champions League campaign, a 1-0 loss to Werder Bremen when their passage to the knockout phase was all but assured, and the received wisdom was that, for Liverpool to have any chance of overcoming them again, an away goal would have to be secured in Stamford Bridge. But the Reds were poor in the first leg and were possibly lucky to escape with a 1-0 defeat. Benítez was not happy with the performance and said:

Yes, I was very angry after the first game. I was angry with myself, my staff, and my players because we had not performed. I cannot analyse the future of a player in one or two games, but some players must realise that they are playing for a European Cup Final and for their futures. Things can change quickly and decisions over whether you stay with a top side or leave depend on these next few weeks.'

Rafa was evidently running out of patience with some of his players, and there would be casualties within a few months, but in the interim, the

Spanish manager managed to cajole another top performance from his squad when Chelsea arrived at Anfield brimming with self-confidence. Daniel Agger gave Liverpool a 22nd minute lead and the Reds controlled the game from there on but, perhaps lacking a truly top class striker (a fault that would come back to haunt them in the final), they could not break down an expertly drilled Blues defence. Nerves were shredded as the match ticked agonisingly towards extra time and then penalties. It was now time for Pepe Reina – just as he had a year previously in Cardiff – to show his big game temperament and world class shot stopping ability as he saved spot kicks from Arjen Robben and Geremi to help his side win 4-1 on penalties. The result was vindication for Benítez 's tactics and selection (which had been called into question after the first leg) and Steven Gerrard joyfully exclaimed:

'The first time was special but to do it again after being a goal down against a magnificent squad like Chelsea was fantastic. The manager's tactics were spot on and the players stuck together out there. We crossed that line and stuck together out there. The players fought for every ball together. If we are through to the final it has made all that hard work worthwhile.'

There was also the added bonus of refuting Mourinho's smirking comments – in which the Chelsea manager had dismissed Liverpool as a 'little club' based on their performance over the course of the season. The Portuguese manager's reaction to elimination was hardly magnanimous either as he ludicrously claimed that: 'physically in the second half and extra time we were the only team that tried to win in ninety and one hundred and twenty minutes.' Shorn of a ghost goal to moan about, Mourinho could dwell on his sense of injustice all he liked; Liverpool were in the Champions League Final for the second time in three seasons.

The Milan team that lay in wait in Athens was undoubtedly weaker than the side the Reds had so memorably defeated two years previously and Liverpool – despite possessing flaws – were a more rounded squad than their predecessors. But the final was one of those anticlimactic matches that never really got going and, crucially for them, Milan scored at just the right times with Filippo Inzaghi netting rather fortuitously just before half time and then again in the 82nd minute. The Reds, though, were a trifle workmanlike and lacked that razzmatazz, that cutting edge to really inflict damage on the Milan defence. In hindsight, perhaps it was not the right call to deploy Kuyt – a willing, energetic worker but suspect finisher with any consistency (despite him scoring a late consolation) - ahead of Crouch, who only entered the fray in the 78th minute and immediately started causing havoc. Steven Gerrard didn't enjoy his best night and looked heavy footed and though Jermaine Pennant technically played well, he frequently made poor decisions. As the Italian side celebrated their revenge, it would be churlish to claim they were lucky but the reality was that this was a game that could literally have gone either way; perhaps Milan shaded it but Liverpool had their chances which they just couldn't finish.

A world class finisher would no doubt have made a difference and as Rafa Benítez prepared to face the globe's press the following day, perhaps this was what he had in mind.

CHAPTER 13 - THE GATHERING STORM

On 24th of May 2007, the morning after Liverpool's narrow defeat to Milan in the Champions League Final, Rafa Benítez publically demanded backing in the transfer market from the club's new owners.

'(They) say they will support us, but now is not the time to talk but to take decisions. It's not just about new faces, it's about the structure of the club.'

At the time, the press conference did not garner huge attention and it was more a case of most Liverpool supporters agreeing with the manager. David Moores had initially decided to sell the club because he knew – in the age of the uber squads of Chelsea and Manchester United, when these two financial behemoths could routinely fork out eye-watering fees for average players – that he was no longer able to financially compete. Added to this was the long-mooted move to a new stadium in Stanley Park; a contentious issue and one that would be a huge monetary endeavour. Despite comfortably and routinely finishing in the top four, the Reds had lacked the real muscle to go after the absolute top talent that would transform them into a side capable of mounting a sustained challenge for the Premier League title.

Tom Hicks and George Gillett had acquired Liverpool Football Club the previous February for a fee in the region of £172 million but as far back as 2004, the Reds' board had been looking for investment to help fund the stadium issue and the playing staff. The billionaire prime minister of Thailand, Thaksin Shinawatra, had offered £65 million for a 30% stake in the club while local businessman Steve Morgan had made a counter-offer of a reported £73 million. Both were ultimately rejected; the rising fears about alleged human rights' abuse in Thailand were possibly a major factor in the refusal of Shinawatra's offer while, in Morgan's case, the Liverpool board claimed the offer 'undervalued' the club. Two years later, after tentatively exploring the near sacrilegious notion of sharing a new stadium with Everton, Moores and chief executive Rick Parry were still looking for investment when a consortium representing Dubai International Capital (DIC) made a reported £156 million offer for the club, with additional funds promised for stadium development; the package was said to be around £450 million. Though there were more whisperings of DIC having a less than perfect human rights' record (it is an arm of the Dubai government and its ruling family), the board seemed keen to accept the deal (and apparently Moores had shaken hands on the buyout).

But ultimately Moores and Parry walked away and into the waiting arms of Hicks and Gillett, two American sports and property tycoons who had raised the offer for the club to £172 million, plus promised funds for the development of the stadium.

Speaking on the *The Anfield Wrap* podcast years later, Rick Parry outlined the convoluted take-over and the issues with DIC:

'By December 2006 when they finally come back and say 'here's a deal' and David said it's acceptable, they'd been working with us for 18 months.' (Parry had initially made contact in Istanbul at the 2005 Champions League Final).

'We said there's a transfer window coming up, there is steel to be ordered for the stadium, this all has to be signed, sealed and delivered by the 31st of December. You can't possibly need much time for due diligence because what else is there to do, you've been pouring all over the club for eighteen months, you've got all the financial models. They said that would be fine. As we now know, we then got to February, we'd missed the transfer window, and we'd got really exposed over a steel order.

We had a board meeting in late January 2007 and – it sounds crazy now – but we were racing to get the stadium built, delivered and in place by 2009 and of course, there's a real critical (time) path to do that. And if we were to have any chance of hitting the close season, we were told we had to order the steel, about £10m worth, in the January. And still DIC hadn't completed. And we spoke to their number two guy to try to push things along. We said "we've got a board meeting, we need to discuss the steel order, what's the board to do about the steel?" And he said "we'll underwrite it, don't worry, go ahead, order it and tell the board that DIC is underwriting the steel."

Then literally the next day the boss of DIC says he had no right to say that. And you think, "hang on there's got to be a degree of good faith in this, what is going on?"

We've placed the order, we're exposed and you're saying we had no right to do it and the deal still isn't finalised.

Bearing in mind the pace of Dubai, the growth, the amount they invest when they want something to happen, this wasn't feeling like Dubai and also you're starting to think if it's like this before the deal's done what will it be like afterwards.'

The Liverpool board were getting cold feet and with mounting fears that the deal would not go ahead and with previous deadlines having passed, Moores rang the DIC chair, Sameer al-Ansari, to express their concerns. The apparent response that Moores got from al-Ansari, an almost scathing 'if you don't commit to DIC by 5pm today, we're walking away' finally convinced the Liverpool chairman to change direction.

DIC were furious at the collapse, describing the club as a 'shambles' and the Liverpool board as 'dishonourable.' Moores claimed that 'you're not going to blackmail Liverpool Football Club. No one's going to treat us like that, we'll call your bluff.' The result was that Hicks and Gillett were given practically a free run in the take-over saga but as John Williams noted in *Red Men*:

'Moores might well have favoured passing on his Liverpool shares to the Americans for reason other than profit. After all, these were two identifiable sports benefactors from across the Atlantic, people who understood the global sports business and who had money to invest, but also had the club apparently at heart.'

In short, despite some fears and despite the club going against years of the oft-quoted 'Liverpool Way', the patrician, conservative history of the remnants of the Littlewoods empire, many embraced the idea, particularly when the two Americans played an expert charm offensive to the gallery of Liverpool fans in their numerous interviews with the media. Certainly, it was not viewed with anything like the alarm with which some Manchester United fans greeted the Glazer takeover of their club.

Essentially, Hicks and Gillett turned to the Royal Bank of Scotland to secure the loan they needed to purchase the club: a package which topped £470 million, including the £215 million needed to start work on the new stadium. Unfortunately, the debt was then loaded onto Liverpool's holding company. As Parry said:

'The debt was never on the club because David Moores and I blocked that. It was on the holding company, but clearly they needed to get money from the club to pay the interest so that was going to be a burden. Our clear understanding was that it was a short term debt while they organised their finances. It was in the offer document that there would be no debt on the club, or the club would not have not have to bear the costs, and certainly that changed. We weren't comfortable or happy with that.'

This became apparent early on, but the first official element of refinancing was agreed in January 2008. £105 million of the original debt was lumbered on Liverpool with a further £185 million being secured on Kop Investment LLC, the club's holding company held in the Cayman Islands. Suddenly, this looked like highly risky financial waters and with the new owners having ended their campaign of charm with a very public rebuking of Rafa Benítez, any honeymoon they may have enjoyed was now officially over.

In the interim, and with all this (prior to Hicks' admonishing of Benítez) going on under the radar of many Liverpool fans, it seemed that the Liverpool manager's entreaties to the owners had worked. A welcome flurry of transfer activity saw the arrival of Lucas Leiva, Ryan Babel, Yossi Benayoun and Fernando Torres. This was not the shopping in Primark that Rafa had been forced to rely on mostly; this was heading towards the bright lights and Liverpool fans were delighted with a spend of £45 million on this quartet (also arriving were the stables of Benítez's tenure, the likes of Sebastián Leto, Krisztián Németh and Emiliano Insúa; low fee and low risk, although it has to be noted that many of these transfers added up to a considerable sum). Moreover, another £25 million was spent on Martin Škrtel and Javier Mascherano the following January. But it was the signing of the golden-maned figure of Torres, El Niño, a bona fide world star in the making, that caught many imaginations. Manchester United and Chelsea had long been linked with the Spaniard but it was Benítez who pounced with just over £20 million needed to prise him away from Atlético Madrid in the summer of 2007.

The subsequent season – sandwiched as it was between a Champions League Final and a push at the title – has been slightly forgotten about and certainly underrated. But it was another thrilling campaign with Gerrard (now pushed into a more advanced role) and Torres frequently dovetailing telepathically to devastating effect. The Anfield crowd's introduction to the Spaniard was a 1-1 draw with Chelsea in which El Niño skinned John Terry before planting an angled shot adroitly past Petr Cech. A love affair had begun.

In two games in late August and early September, the Reds scored ten times without reply against Toulouse and a hopelessly out of their depth Derby County. This was the level of Benítez's current side; they were able to routinely hand out hammerings and put teams to the sword and scored at least three goals on eighteen occasions (in all competitions). Reina was cementing himself as one of the best goalkeepers on the planet, the technically excellent if sometimes brittle Daniel Agger forged a superb partnership with Jamie Carragher (with Škrtel and Hyypiä providing suitable top class cover) and ahead of them Javier Mascherano was rapidly proving himself to be one of the best defensive midfielders in world football. Though Alonso did not enjoy his best season for the Reds (prompting the first incipient stirrings of interest in Gareth Barry by Benítez, a dalliance that would fatally undermine the Spaniard's relationship with his manager), he was still capable of producing frequent moments of absolute quality. This formidable spine was tipped by Gerrard – now operating at the peak of his daunting powers – and Torres, who settled in Liverpool seamlessly and scored a total of thirty three goals. There was, quite simply, top class talent throughout the pitch and a supporting cast that included Kuyt, Benayoun, Crouch, Babel, Riise and Arbeloa graphically portrays the expertise with which Benítez had patiently assembled his squad.

But a title challenge in the 2007/08 season never really looked likely as this team needed another campaign to completely mature together. Liverpool would finish fourth but they could point to more progress and consolidation as the gap to champions Manchester United was eleven points by the time the season ended. However, Benítez was under pressure. In October of 2007, a 2-1 away defeat to Besiktas had left the Reds staring grimly at early elimination from the Champions League. Compounding this, it later transpired that during November – with Liverpool's immediate European future looking bleak – Hicks had met with Jürgen Klinsmann with a view to replacing Benítez (adding to the fuel that was causing a fire of civil war to wage was the American owner telling the manager to 'concentrate on training and coaching the players he already has'; a declaration that prompted Benítez to frostily repeat the phrase in a press conference).

Ostensibly, Hicks claimed that the courting of the German manager was 'an insurance policy, to have him become manager if Rafa left for Real Madrid' but the battle lines had been drawn and mobilisation was rapidly occurring. By January 2008, with rumours swirling that DIC were about to re-enter the fray with a £500 million offer, the Spirit of Shankly supporter group was formed, and they led the protests against the ownership of the Americans. The supporters were clearly behind Rafa as Kopites carried a homemade banner to a 2-2 Anfield draw with Aston Villa bearing words that could hardly have been more stark: 'Yanks out, Dubai in. In Rafa we love.'

This, then, was the backdrop upon which a season-defining few games were played out by Benítez's charges. Liverpool's interest in the Champions League was maintained beyond Christmas by a series of staggering displays – just when the knives appeared to be out for the manager at board room level. Needing three victories from their final three games to have any hope of advancing from their group, the Reds trounced Besiktas 8-0 (a Champions League record until Benítez himself broke it with Real Madrid in 2015), Porto 4-1 and finally a 4-0 obliteration of Marseille at the Stade Vélodrome in France.

Inter Milan were then defeated comprehensively over two legs by an aggregate score of 3-0 before a monumental clash with Arsenal in the quarter-finals of UEFA's flagship competition. Dirk Kuyt equalised Emmanuel Adebayor's opener for the Gunners to give the Reds a vital away goal. The Anfield tie was a topsy-turvy, nerve-shredding affair in what was now becoming almost routinely memorable European nights under Benítez. In the 84th minute, with Liverpool winning 2-1 on the night, Theo Walcott ran practically the length of the pitch to cross for a simple finish for Adebayor, giving Arsenal the lead on away goals. Collectively, the Anfield crowd still had their heads in their hands, almost expecting the worst (although fightbacks had obviously been a characteristic of Rafa's

Reds), when Ryan Babel – so often a figure of frustration but one who still had big moments for Liverpool – won a penalty for his side after tormenting Kolo Touré. Steven Gerrard gave Liverpool the lead and it was the Dutch youngster who fired in a 90th minute fourth to finally settle the anxieties of the home crowd.

Liverpool's reward for reaching yet another Champions League Semi-Final (their third in four years, making them UEFA's top ranking side) was the now annual double header with Chelsea. With the Blues now shorn of José Mourinho after the Portuguese had been fired following a spell of indifferent but hardly calamitous form, Benítez was denied the chance of a personal hat-trick of successful duels in the European arena. Nevertheless, this was still an intimidating Chelsea outfit and when a catastrophic 90th minute own goal from Riise gave the Londoners an ill-deserved 1-1 draw at Anfield, Kopites feared the worse. The return leg was another classic but this time, for once, the Reds fell just short. With Fernando Torres forcing extra time with a 64th minute equaliser to Didier Drogba's opener, Frank Lampard then scored a penalty and the Ivorian sealed the win with a 105th minute strike. Briefly, Ryan Babel's thunderbolt gave the Reds hope but it was just too little, too late. Another epic then, but this time Liverpool had to swallow the bitter medicine of defeat in a pulsating encounter.

But this medicine was not half as unpleasant as the revelations that were emerging from the Liverpool boardroom at around the same time that the players and manager were involved in such epic battles on the field of play. In April, it became clear that Hicks and Gillett were no longer on speaking terms and barely communicated and, indeed, could barely agree on the future of the football club. Gillett appeared as if he may be about to sell his share of Liverpool, possibly to DIC, while Hicks, in typically public fashion, came out and claimed that Rick Parry was 'failing' (it also became apparent that Parry had been at the meeting with Klinsmann, thus further souring his relationship with Benítez). A club long built on conservatism and stability, on the Liverpool Way of dignity and respect, of insularity (sometimes lapsing into self-indulgence), was now a laughing stock as the loan leveraged on the club was said to be approaching £313 million.

It was about to get grimmer for beleaguered fans but the eye of the storm still cast a translucent light that flickered all too briefly. Rafa had one more special season ahead with his Liverpool side.

CHAPTER 14 - THE BOY FROM MADRID

Let's briefly fast forward a few years to a spring evening in 2015. It was then, during a charity game between a Steven Gerrard XI and a Jamie Carragher XI, that there seemed to be an excising of something malignant and treacherous that Liverpool fans had carried in their hearts for four years.

This was a match where former heroes said goodbye, and as the likes of Xabi Alonso, Pepe Reina and Luis Suárez applauded a bouncing, if poignantly existential, Anfield, for one footballer the emotion appeared to be threatening to overwhelm him. Fernando Torres, now a man of thirty one – not the spritely and shining demigod of eight years previous – was visibly overcome as the Kop sang his name. It was a crystallising catharsis as El Niño had to compose himself as his name drifted from the stands in a chorus of stoic gratitude. Torres applauded and there was a look of something not far removed from shock in his eyes. Shock and thankfulness.

Because it had hurt. January 2011 had hurt more than football really should. It hurt because we cared so much, worshipped this mercurial and prolific striker who seemed to get us, our club, our city. The irony of course being that it was this sense of loss, of betrayal, that ensured that, for many Liverpool fans, Torres would be the last of the heroes; never again would we leave ourselves open to the deathly keen blade of loss that we felt when Chelsea signed him for £50 million. He wanted the move, he was disillusioned with the mess our club had become. So he jumped ship to the hated Londoners and it was horribly emblematic of just how much modern football had changed, taking us with it. We would indulge in a strange voyeurism as we watched Chelsea's new striker struggle in a side based around patient possession and some would delight in it while some would feel a strange ache – like meeting a hot ex-partner in a club who has obviously lost much of what gave them their power over you. Vivacity traded for vacuity.

But the glorious memories would always remain. They could be hidden away as we nursed our outrage at being jilted and bruised but maybe, during a friendly that was an unofficial goodbye to Steven Gerrard (so many goodbyes), we could all take part in a group therapy session and remember that we were privileged to witness one of the greatest strikers on the planet plying his trade at Anfield.

In 'Champions League Dreams', Rafa Benítez had written about his pursuit of Torres:

We knew, despite the presence of Dirk Kuyt and Peter Crouch, that if we were to progress as a club, we needed to make at least one headline signing, to capture a player that would make the rest of Europe sit up and take notice … we dissected some of the biggest names in European football until we had our one … (Torres) would become, at the time, the most expensive signing in Liverpool's history. But we knew we had found the player we wanted, we needed. He had pace, he was good in the air and, most of all, he had tremendous hunger, to improve himself, to win trophies.'

For his part, the Spanish striker wrote in his autobiography of the sense of inexorable fate which led him to Anfield.

When I was playing for Atletico Madrid against Real Sociedad I was battling with a defender and the captain's armband I was wearing came loose and fell open. As it hung from my arm, you could see the message written on the inside, in English: "We'll Never Walk Alone" … an eagle eyed photographer spotted the picture and I was immediately linked to Liverpool.'

It should be noted here that the legend emblazoned on the inside of the armband had nothing to do with Liverpool. It was a gesture between his close friends – not uncommon is Spain – in which they had all committed to getting a tattoo to highlight their solidarity. Torres was aware of the connotations to Anfield and didn't wish to show disrespect to his employers and so they had settled on this method. At least this was the claim of the striker. But, regardless, Torres went on:

'Maybe that was the day I took my first step towards Anfield, or maybe it was because I already shared things with Liverpool. I identify with the values that define the club: hard work, struggle, humility, effort, tenacity, commitment, togetherness, unity, faith, the permanent desire to improve, to overcome all obstacles.'

It really did look like being a match made in heaven, though there was the lingering sense that Torres was a scorer of great goals rather than a great goalscorer. However, in his debut season in a red shirt, he showed himself to be both as he cut a swathe through defences home and abroad. That dizzying, dazzling smile, that sprint away – sometimes sliding to his knees, at other times both hands raised to his adoring public, these images were burned onto our consciousness during his debut season. Lightning quick, courageous, a fine finisher with either foot, possessed of a keen footballing mind and an accomplished header of the ball, El Niño captured the imagination of all and sundry. Records were set to tumble.

In thirty three league games in the 07/08 season, Torres scored twenty four goals, becoming the first Liverpool player since Robbie Fowler to score twenty or more in the league, and a record in a debut season for a foreign striker. In early 2008, he became the first Liverpool player since Jackie Balmer (over fifty years previously) to score successive Anfield hat-tricks versus Middlesbrough and West Ham. His winner against Manchester City on 4th May, 2008 meant that Torres had equalled Roger Hunt's long standing club record of scoring in eight consecutive league games at Anfield.

It is not hyperbole to suggest that – even after just one season – the Spanish striker was well on the way to joining the great pantheon of post-war Liverpool centre forwards; footballers ensconced firmly in legend such as Hunt, Rush, Fowler and Owen. It was a genuine love affair as Anfield consistently rocked to the beat of Torres' unique gifts. And the adoration that emanated with a tangible authenticity from the stands appeared to be reciprocated by El Niño. He completely got our club and the Liverpool way of life and, from the off, immersed himself in the storied history of the club, consuming books and DVDs with a relentless drive that was matched only by his goal scoring. Early on in his Liverpool career, he had dinner with Anfield luminaries Kenny Dalglish, Sammy Lee and Graeme Souness. He gobbled it all up with a cold eyed and single natured ferocity and he genuinely seemed to have found a new spiritual home. As the Spaniard said in a newspaper interview in 2009:

There are similar characteristics between playing for Atletico and playing for Liverpool – at the club and with the people in the street. Liverpool is a working class city, the people work hard all week and then try to be happy with the football at the weekend, so it's very similar to Madrid. I was born in a working class town in the suburbs of Madrid and Atletico was the poor team in the city – the small one, next to a massive club like Real Madrid. It's difficult to live like this but it makes you stronger.'

Nor was this symbiosis limited solely to the city; Torres was nearly as appreciative of his manager – at a time when the owners were palpably less so – as most Reds, further cementing his legend amongst Kopites. He would claim that Benítez was responsible for him attaining a level of performance that he had previously never thought possible. Before that first sparkling season in English football, Torres' previous best goals return had been twenty (six of which were penalties) in 2003/04. But from the moment he skinned the Chelsea defence on his Anfield debut, the Spanish striker claimed he just knew his first campaign would be a prolific one; his qualities were ideally suited to the frenetic nature of the domestic game and he was the spear tip in a machine which had been expertly drilled by Benítez. As he told *Four Four Two*:

'I was so confident and comfortable: I could see that I was part of a very well organised team, I could already see that the style of football suited me and that I would get lots of chances.'

With his manager's obsessive attention to detail and drive to perfect this humming engine, the results were spectacular; Torres had the raw physical gifts but it was that perfect marriage with the pragmatic and forensic Rafa that ensured that these talents would bear remarkable fruit.

'I've been lucky enough to have a coach like Rafa Benítez who tries to make you better every single day. There's no doubt I've improved … Some players have to be pushed and piqued, others have to be looked after. When I've scored two or three goals, he tells me I've played badly, that I didn't help out at the back ….'

In short, everything – even his manager's style, which irked some players – just came together to produce a perfect storm of goal scoring finesse that Liverpool fans witnessed for three years. All relationships have a shelf life and even if Chelsea hadn't cast flirtatious eyes at El Niño, the impression nearing the end of his time in a red shirt was that perhaps the affair had run its course. Torres wouldn't be the last Liverpool player of that era to complain of promises that weren't kept by a ruinous regime. But for those three years, Torres lit up the footballing lives of Liverpool fans everywhere. It may be an understandable defence mechanism to almost airbrush some of his escapades from our memories but even a cursory glance through YouTube will remind you of just how special he was in front of goal.

Goals from everywhere. From every angle, bullet-like long range finishes, shots swept into the net from inside the box, towering headers, slaloming dribbles followed by adroit pokes at goal. Defenders routinely and visibly wilted on a football pitch when Torres was at his peak in a red shirt. His trademark drop of a shoulder and curling shot to the far post disguised the fact that frequently the forward would leave a centre-back choking dust as he moved inside before opening up his body and sweeping home. He was practically unplayable at times and if injury hampered his Liverpool career – and there was sometimes a sense of brittleness about the striker – perhaps that was natural selection evening the playing field.

Because Torres was that good; for perhaps two years the best striker in world football.

We will never forget how he left, how we felt and the hollow knell of betrayal deep inside us. Torres said some things he shouldn't have when he swanned off to London – make no mistake about that. He never gave Dalglish a chance really, never got to play with Suárez. But there was a pall over the club; a quagmire that was sucking all that was good from

Liverpool, a cloud of listless lattitude that refused to let the sun penetrate its suffocating denseness. Torres left and it was the romance, that synergetic dance with Liverpool supporters that died that day when he skipped away into the clutches of a hated rival.

But maybe we can now forgive. Not forget; never forget. Never forget what Torres brought to Liverpool. Don't let how it ended ruin what was a miraculous marriage between special fans and a special player. The lingering sense of betrayal will always remain but that's the unfortunate face of this brave new world that is modern football. With other footballers, we have now learned to savour them while they're at Liverpool and this is also part of Torres' legacy.

It is also a legacy of celebration and adoration, of perfect timing and genius level goal scoring. That warm evening in Anfield when it felt – yet again – that Liverpool Football Club was reaching a tipping point, that things needed resolution quickly to prevent falling further behind, when there was a velvet and painful poignancy in the air as so many of our heroes walked the hallowed turf once more. A reflective and accepting mood in a stadium that Torres had graced in a red shirt showed that we have forgiven and that a collective salving catharsis has settled over us all. We should celebrate our former heroes, while glorying in the prospect of more to come.

CHAPTER 15 - ON THE BRINK

As the 2008/09 season dawned, a strange atmosphere surrounded Liverpool Football Club. The hugely disturbing and disrupting noise in the background continued to gather pace and there was a veritable split in the ranks of the fan base. Whereas previously there had been massive support for Benítez in the face of practically untenable conditions, there was now the spectre of civil war – not just in the boardroom, but also on the terraces. While the Liverpool manager retained the support of the majority of fans, there was now an increasingly dissident voice at Anfield; a voice that would not be quieted and, despite evidence to the contrary on the pitch in the campaign to come, would lie in wait and eventually become deafening.

There had long been a crusade waged by the British media – one you might charitably describe as verging on xenophobic – against Rafa Benítez. The facile bleating of some of the more exposed members of this august body had unfortunately filtered down to some of the fan base and a number of myths had become taken as gospel. As Paul Tomkins noted in *Dynasty*:

'visionaries in life – be they in sport, art, music or politics – tend to be more greatly appreciated retrospectively, when their ideas have proven inspired and their influence can be traced.'

What cannot be argued with is that Benítez had delivered a Champions League trophy and the FA Cup, was about to achieve his second eighty-plus points total in four years and had made the Reds the number one ranked side in European competition.

However, it is only fair to note that Benítez's signings – and, indeed, transfer targets – in the summer of 2008 did not help with the rupturing support and was cognitive confirmation writ large for those who had been spoon-fed by the likes of Sky Sports. All managers get transfers wrong, it is a simple fact of managerial life, but what was for many the final nail in the coffin of their allegiance to the Liverpool manager was his pursuit of Gareth Barry at the potential expense of universal fan favourite Xabi Alonso. The Spanish playmaker had not enjoyed his best campaign for the Reds in 2007/08 and had been haunted by injury and loss of form. Barry – a competent and steady professional – was rated highly by Benítez and it looked like the deal was all but done just prior to the 08/09 campaign kicking off. But when the Liverpool manager let it be known that he would be willing to listen to offers for Alonso in order to secure the Villa midfielder, this gave all of his detractors all the ammunition needed to accuse Rafa of indulging in hasty (and premature, as Barry stayed put in the Midlands) crassness. Moreover, within a year of this episode, Xabi Alonso was a Real Madrid player, having just enjoyed arguably his finest season in a red shirt.

A transfer target that was successfully concluded was the signing of Robbie Keane from Tottenham Hotspur for a fee in the region of £20 million. This would prove to be one of those rare occasions were Rafa spent relatively big only for the move to not work out; within a few months the Republic of Ireland forward was on his way back to Spurs, though Liverpool recouped most of their considerable outlay.

It's hard to say what Benítez was hoping to get from Keane, who was more comfortable in a number 10 role behind a striker – a role that Steven Gerrard had pretty much made his own as he gloriously dovetailed with the undisputed first choice striker, Fernando Torres. Possibly the Liverpool manager was hoping to subtly tweak the Irishman's game (after all, Rafa had proved adept at this with many footballers) and did try to get Keane to make differing runs but it was clearly not working. It could well be a case of that intangible and opaque phenomenon when certain players just don't – for a variety of reasons – work out at a club. Perhaps Keane was just too far along his own path as a footballer to be moulded sufficiently by his manager and he also may have been trying too hard in playing for his self-confessed boyhood club. But it became apparent fairly quickly that Benítez had to cut his losses (in order to keep said losses to a minimum) and in the following January the forward returned to Spurs. The Liverpool manager may have thought that there was a replacement lined up but this never materialised as events behind the scenes were quickly unravelling. The upshot of all this of course was that, just when Rafa looked to have assembled a squad replete with genuine talent and world class ability, he lacked effective cover for the sometimes injury-prone Torres (David N'Gog had also arrived but would never really convince).

John-Arne Riise departed the club for Roma and was replaced with the £7 million purchase of Andrea Dossena from Udinese, a player who failed utterly at the club. Chronically lacking the prerequisites to succeed in the Premier League such as height, pace, positional sense and a final ball, the Italian sank without trace (save for still memorable cameos at home to Real Madrid and four days later away to Manchester United in March 2009). This signing was worryingly symptomatic of that particular summer's transfer business; at a time when Rafa needed a top player to supplement the world class spine he had assembled, every one of the transfers from the summer of 2008 ultimately failed to deliver.

Despite all this – and, almost paradoxically made all the more heart-breaking for it – the Reds very nearly had a truly memorable campaign in 2008/09, coming so close to winning that elusive Premier League. This was a side with genuine quality all over the pitch and was arguably the most balanced Liverpool team seen since the club were last champions of England. The brilliant Reina, he of top class saves and even better distribution, with Carragher – now a genuine top performer and one who supplied a Scouse heartbeat – and Agger or Škrtel alongside him. Flanking these was Arbeloa and Aurelio, solid full-backs and decent going forward (if slightly injury-prone in the case of the latter). But it was the midfield and attack where the Reds could compete with most squads in world football. The snarling Mascherano and cultured Alonso complemented each other perfectly with Gerrard, now playing some of the best football of his career, just slightly forward behind the lightening quick and deadly Torres. Albert Riera would also supply some great showings in his one good season in England while the clever, diminutive and skilful Benayoun increasingly came to the fore as the season progressed. It was Benítez's great misfortune that – just when he had a side capable of attacking brilliance on their day – he came up against a Manchester United who were not only used to winning titles (and with a manager arguably at the peak of his formidable powers) but also possessed one of the greatest forward lines in recent history with Ronaldo – now resembling some kind of footballing Robocop – ably assisted by Tevez, Rooney and Berbatov.

The Reds would only suffer two defeats in the entire league season, unluckily to Tottenham in Harry Redknapp's first game in charge and then to Middlesbrough in late February. The latter game graphically showed the paucity in Liverpool's squad depth, as, shorn of Fernando Torres, Benítez called on Nabil El Zhar to replace him. We can't – even now – know the full rumblings of what was transpiring behind the scenes but it's probably safe to make the claim that all of the upheaval had had a negative effect on targets that Rafa had prioritised; he was, in effect, hamstrung, fatally so in relation to the Premier League title.

Moreover, the sense that recruitment (or lack thereof) fatally undermined the challenge can be explicitly attested to by even a cursory glance at the costly draws, particularly at home, against sides that Liverpool would expect to beat with the minimum of fuss. By the time the Reds drew

2-2 at Anfield with Hull City ('No Torres, no knockout,' screamed *The Echo*'s headlines), Benítez's charges had already dropped six points at home to Stoke, Fulham and West Ham. That boos rang out from some sections of a frustrated support at a result that saw Liverpool go top of the Premier League table was typical of the fissures that were now stretching through the terraces; no longer – despite some sterling performances and overwhelming evidence that the Spaniard deserved better – was every Kopite behind the manager.

And sterling performances from this gifted group of players there were, none more so than hitting eight goals in a few days against Real Madrid and Manchester United in the Champions League and Premier League respectively, the latter blowing open the title race and for the first time sowing a seed of doubt in Manchester's collective consciousness. These epic results took place amid another tumultuous backdrop, with rumours swirling that Benítez was about to quit the club and with Tom Hicks publicly demanding that Rick Parry, who was, so the American claimed, 'failing,' resign. David Moores would announce himself as disgusted with the treatment of Parry and in June of 2009 – mere weeks after Liverpool had so nearly won the league – would retire from the Liverpool board, announcing that he was 'heartbroken' at how Hicks and Gillett had treated his beloved Liverpool.

John Williams captured the unravelling horror of many Liverpool supporters at what was transpiring as their side looked to beat the odds in the late spring of 2009:

'At the same time, Merseyside MPs called for the British government to resist an application from the Americans for a loan of £350 million from the majority government owned Royal Bank of Scotland. Liverpool Football Club, once a model of conservative and unobtrusive stability in the English game, suddenly seemed to be impossibly split, rudderless and constantly in the public eye.'

But still, with all this distraction, it was a case of what may have been in both the league and in Europe. The Reds put in a fine effort in both arenas but ultimately just fell short. After the aforementioned demoralising defeat to Middlesbrough at the Riverside – a loss that seemed to have put Liverpool out of realistic contention for the league in late February – the Reds then took thirty one points from the remaining thirty three; only failing to win in the epic 4-4 Anfield draw with Arsenal. In the European campaign, the Reds had given a typically fine display – crushing Real Madrid 5-0 on aggregate along the way – before bowing out to Chelsea in the last eight, notwithstanding a hugely spirited 4-4 draw at Stamford Bridge.

However, despite these near misses, and regardless of the storm clouds of civil war and troubling financial rumours that continued to hover in the background, many Liverpool supporters were guardedly upbeat in the summer of 2009. Indeed, even the fickle mainstream media now appeared behind Benítez and, prior to the 2009/10 season, the Reds were seen by many as the favourites for the Premier League title. Nevertheless, Christian Purslow, a financial expert, was appointed as a condition of yet another loan, and his brief was to find £100 million worth of investment. According to Rafa, he would be present at every press conference and loitering at every interview. The vultures, it would appear, were still circling. Xabi Alonso was sold to Real Madrid for £30 million with Benítez having identified the Italian Alberto Aquilani as his replacement. The Roma midfielder was plagued by a serious injury and the Liverpool manager sought the advice of three different surgeons who, apparently, gave three different time periods for his recovery which ranged from a month to three months. It would actually be four months before the Italian was ready to take his place in training and, as Rafa himself said, 'even then, it was impossible to push him too much in training, as he was still hampered slightly by the after effects of the injury.' With Arbeloa also heading to the Spanish capital, Glen Johnson arrived for a fairly hefty £17.5 million. He was a more offensive option than his predecessor and, though recent years may have told us otherwise, for three seasons he was one of the best attacking right-backs in the league.

Along with the sales of Sebastián Leto, Dossena and Andriy Voronin for a combined fee of nearly £10 million, this meant that Liverpool should have had substantial funds still available for a striker and a centre-back. Benítez had identified Stevan Jovetic to boost his striking options and either Matthew Upson or Sylvain Distin as cover in defence. But as the Liverpool manager wrote himself:

'Liverpool, though, was no longer a football club. It was a business. We were told, long after we had drawn up our plans, that we had spent all the money available to us … I kept asking questions of Purslow, of the owners, and they would not give me answers. I could have guessed what had happened, of course, but their silence spoke volumes. The money which we wanted to us to take Liverpool to the next level was gone.'

In the end, far from sign players of genuine excitement who may have helped Liverpool consolidate and maybe kick on, Benítez had to settle for the cut price Sotirios Kyrgiakos, a whole-hearted but lumbering, one-paced centre-back.

It may be tempting to lay the blame for the calamity that was the 09/10 campaign solely at the feet of Hicks and Gillett but it was not quite as clear cut (even if it's even more appealing to indulge in what may have been; imagine Jovetic and Upson signed and the season got off to a better start). But Liverpool fans have seen the cost of a huge push for the title and the subsequent hangover that sets in more than once since the formation of the Premier League. It could be argued that the gargantuan force of will required, the massive effort expanded, left the players – both physically and psychologically – some way short of peak condition. Moreover, what cannot be denied in modern football is that managers often have a shelf life; a period of time where their ideas are fresh and respected. Success helps, of course, but after a certain amount of time has elapsed, sometimes it's hard to stop the rot from setting in over the squad. Liverpool possessed two players in their squad who wielded huge power – not just in the dressing room but within the very fabric of the club itself. Steven Gerrard and Jamie Carragher had, for example, been consulted with plans for the mirage that was the new stadium and had often been asked to identify transfer targets. Once they were something less than onside with the manager, he was always fighting an uphill battle. The cancerous malaise that had no doubt started with the mess at boardroom level was starting to multiply and spread throughout every facet of Liverpool Football Club as poison and malignant cells sprang up everywhere.

In September of 2009, as the Reds struggled with an underwhelming start to a campaign that had appeared to promise so much, George Gillett met with the supporter group Spirit of Shankly. Here he criticised the manager and claimed that Liverpool's financial situation was healthier than Manchester United's. He also, almost surreally, denied promising prompt work on the new stadium. A few months later, with the Reds having been eliminated from the Champions League and languishing in seventh – fourteen points behind table-topping Chelsea – Tom Hicks' son was forced to resign following a tirade by email against a fan which saw Ian Ayre, the club's commercial director, added to the board.

League form was inconsistent with Torres – sometimes looking like he was being forced to play through an injury by his beleaguered manager – appearing increasingly disillusioned. By the end of April, Liverpool were knocked out of the UEFA Cup at the semi-final stage by an extra time Diego Forlán goal and were effectively out of the running for even fourth place in the Premier League. Now, without more European glory to act as a reprieve, Rafa Benítez could hear the sharpening of the executioner's blade. Martin Broughton, the chairman of British Airways, was then brought in by Hicks and Gillett to oversee the sale of the club. A statement from the Americans read:

'Owning Liverpool Football Club over these past three years has been an exciting and rewarding experience for us and our families. Having grown the Club this far we have now decided together to look to sell the Club to owners committed to take the Club through its next level of growth and development.'

As incredulous supporters read this sham of a statement, delivered apparently without a tongue wedged in a cheek, it became apparent that the end game was in sight. But we still didn't know just how bad things had got and that there would still be another massive casualty of this toxic regime.

CHAPTER 16 - DARKEST NIGHTS AND FALSE DAWNS

The autumn and winter months of 2010 will never be remembered fondly by any Liverpool fans. Indeed, the twin H bombs of Heysel and Hillsborough notwithstanding, there was probably never a more depressing time to call yourself a Red, and certainly not since the formation of the Premier League. Even the frustration and relative fallowness of the Souness years paled in comparison with those dark months. Atypically for the terraces of Anfield, with a crowd mobilised further, if not in unity, then certainly in a common cause of hatred for the owners of the club, by October the new Liverpool manager was being castigated mercilessly as he haplessly rubbed his face and made vainglorious excuses. Results on the pitch plummeted to new lows while affairs away from the actual football were equally depressing as the club's very existence was briefly threatened.

Despite retaining a hugely loyal cadre of fans, Rafa Benítez had also become a divisive figure on the terraces by the summer of 2010 and had lost the support of two of the most influential members of the playing squad. With the toxic friction that was the Spaniard's relationship with an increasingly convoluted board room, and following a disappointing campaign that had seen the Reds finish seventh in the Premier League, Benítez was never going to survive the chop. On June 3rd Liverpool announced that he would leave the club 'by mutual consent.' Recently appointed chairman, Martin Broughton, who would now be tasked with finding a replacement as his bosses sought to sell the club, said:

'Rafa will forever be part of Liverpool folklore after bringing home the Champions League following the epic final in Istanbul, but after a disappointing season both parties felt a fresh start would be best for all concerned.'

This less than ebullient and effusive epitaph was emblematic of the corrosively erroneous view of Benítez that was held by many within the media and, evidently, those within the corridors of power at Anfield. He had taken a club on its knees and made them the most feared side in Europe within the space of a few years. Dion Fanning, writing in *The Independent*, prophetically declared that Liverpool supporters would look back at the Spaniard's tenure as a golden age and, even though there was a deeply fractured fan base during his reign, few Reds with even a smattering of footballing knowledge would now dispute this prescient prediction.

Broughton's choice to fill Benítez's shoes was the clichéd steady hands of a much travelled but respected English coach, Roy Hodgson, who had garnered much domestic respect by improbably getting his Fulham side to the UEFA Cup Final, where they had been beaten by Atlético Madrid. It was enough to secure him an LMA manager of the year award and, on the Liverpool board's part, a catastrophically myopic move to the Reds. Hindsight may well be a boon to all football experts, but the infinitely pragmatic Hodgson's success had been built on uninspiring football and securing survival. Fine for the likes of the Cottagers, but expectations at Liverpool are on a wholly different level. Sure, he had won titles in the relative footballing backwater of Scandinavia but, even here, his methods had been more about grinding than decisive football. When he had been given big jobs – Internazionale of Milan and a then still-flush Blackburn Rovers – the results had been borderline disastrous.

And so it would prove at Liverpool. On the face of it, Joe Cole was the new manager's first signing, but it was a transfer that had the grubby fingerprints of managing director Christian Purslow all over it. Cole was joined by Paul Konchesky and Christian Poulsen in a troika of mediocrity to rival the summer of 2002's horrendous transfer dealings. Brad Jones and Raul Meireles were also recruited; the former would still be claiming a wage at the club six years later while the latter was one of Hodgson's better signings but still barely lasted a year. To make matters worse – and in fairness to the new manager, this was hardly his fault – Mascherano effectively downed tools and went on strike after Barcelona started casting flirtatious looks in his direction. By 30th August he would sign for the Catalans, robbing Hodgson of one of the best defensive midfielders in the game. The woefully one-paced and insipid Poulsen was hardly a replacement in the Reds' engine room.

Things never really got going for Roy Hodgson in the Liverpool dug out. Certainly, the so-called coup that was Joe Cole (later to be memorably, and with waspish scouse humour, christened 'Joke Hole') getting sent off in his first game (a decent 1-1 draw with Arsenal in the opening league game) in a red shirt didn't help and there were other mitigating circumstances. Fernando Torres clearly never bought into the new project and soon his away performances of the previous campaign were the norm. The Spaniard was patently disillusioned with promises that had been made and then broken and looked a shadow of the player that had terrorised defenders throughout Europe. Added to this, there was never any real affection for the new manager as there was still a significant residual support for the departed Benítez and, moreover, there was a ready-made replacement – and club legend – in the looming Dalglish, who still stalked the halls of Anfield. It was notably said that using Torres in the manner Hodgson did was like using a Ferrari to plough a field.

The fanbase was splintered, seething with fury at the shambles that was going on behind the scenes, and patience was in short supply. Liverpool supporters were in no mood to listen to the posturing of a besieged manager whose sound bites added to the conviction that he was just not up to the challenge. In short, it wouldn't take much for the atmosphere to truly turn noxious and, along with the feeling that clearly Hodgson never 'got' the club, it meant that a poor start to the season would be accompanied by the hammering sound of a gallows being constructed.

And, make no mistake, the first few months of the 2010/11 campaign were truly awful. After the encouraging 1-1 Anfield draw with Arsenal, the Reds were systematically destroyed 3-0 by newly minted Manchester City. Pepe Reina was then man of the match in an utterly uninspiring 0-0 draw with Birmingham City which was followed by a 3-2 defeat at the hands of Manchester United. The Reds had come from 2-0 down to equalise through a Steven Gerrard free kick only to see Berbatov agonisingly hit an overhead kick winner. It was a familiar theme; hope plucked away just when we hoped a corner may be in sight. In a season of apparent nadirs, the next calamity was a 2-2 draw, followed by a shootout elimination, against Fourth Division Northampton Town in the League Cup ('they'll be a formidable challenge,' Hodgson had infamously quipped prior to the game). This depressing litany continued as newly promoted Blackpool departed Anfield with a 2-1 victory as the first incipient chants for Dalglish to replace Hodgson cascaded from the terraces as the King himself looked on from the Main Stand. By the time Everton routinely defeated the Reds 2-0 in the next league game ('that was as good as we have played all season and I have no qualms with the performance whatsoever,' claimed the manager), it was clear that he was now fighting a losing battle.

Not that Hodgson himself had any doubts about his ability to manage one of Europe's biggest clubs. Just prior to the woeful capitulation by his charges in the derby – and with the writing clearly on the wall – the manager had unconvincingly told the assembled media in cringe-inducing style that:

' ... it would be a sad day for football and for Liverpool if someone who had been brought in with the pomp and circumstance, and the money it took them to release me

from my previous contract, and being feted as one of England's best managers – if after eight games people are deciding this guy has got to go. It would be sad for me. These things happen in football. You can't have the years in football I've had without ever being sacked, but it would be a sad day for Liverpool because that isn't Liverpool's style. So I find that type of question insulting to me and even more insulting to the club.'

A few weeks before this, in what would come to be seen as the definitive Hodgson quote of his time with Liverpool, he had surreally claimed that his management methods had translated 'from Halmstad to Malmö to Örebro to Neuchâtel Xamax to the Swiss national team', apparently blissfully unaware that Liverpool Football Club was a far different beast. His ingratiating himself to Alex Ferguson and saying 'we will cross that bridge when we come to it' concerning the potential sale of Torres, were merely further nails in the coffin of his Anfield career. It was, undeniably, a match made in footballing hell, and after the aforementioned derby defeat, Liverpool were languishing in nineteenth place and firmly entrenched in what looked like a relegation battle unless dramatic changes were made.

As if all this wasn't disturbing enough for Liverpool supporters, there was also the little matter of the club's ownership and in October, in a case that received huge national and international coverage, representatives of the Liverpool board set off for the High Court in London.

CHAPTER 17 - THE END OF THE STORM?

'... an epic swindle at the hands of rogue corporate directors, Broughton, Ayre and Purslow, who considered to sell the iconic Liverpool Football Club at a price they know to be hundreds of millions of dollars below the true market value.'

Tom Hicks and George Gillett, October 2010.

The trip to the High Court in London, as media cameras descended and supporter groups such as Spirit of Shankly anxiously and breathlessly demonstrated outside, has become the stuff of grim legend in our recent past. But like all legends, myths have sprung up to replace facts and in this tangled and convoluted legal minefield, it has been forgotten by some that it was actually the hated American owners – Tom Hicks and George Gillett – who initiated, at least indirectly, the visit to London.

In 2007, following a refinancing of the loan from Royal Bank of Scotland, the bank had insisted that Martin Broughton be brought in with essentially one role: to sell the club. Effectively what it now meant was that Broughton, together with his fellow directors Ian Ayre and Christian Purslow, could outvote their bosses in a decision to sell the club once a reasonable offer had been received. Hicks and Gillett felt that the club was worth between £450 million and £600 million and vaguely claimed to have possible buyers lined up who were willing to shell out these eye-watering sums. But Broughton – club chairman since early in 2010 – and his two directorial allies had accepted a £300 million offer from New England Sports Ventures, a US conglomerate led by John Henry and Tom Warner. So it was that on the 12th of October, as results on the pitch went from bad to worse, the two Americans who had so ineptly run Liverpool Football Club had an injunction taken against them by the RBS to prevent them from changing the constitution of the board.

How bad could it have got? This was firmly in the realms of legality; sentiment and affection had no place in the halls of the High Court and the judges would act solely within their legal remit. As John Williams put it in his peerless chronicle of the history of the club, *Red Men*:

'If the NESV purchase of Liverpool had been legally blocked by Hicks and Gillett, it was still possible that Liverpool FC could have ended up being owned by the publicly funded RBS (whose loan was still outstanding and due to be settled on 15

October) and/or could even be docked nine points by the Premier League for falling into administration by dint of being unable to repay the debts acquired under the inept leadership of Hicks and Gillett. What this Kafka-like state of affairs meant was that the future of this previously commercially and culturally successful and rather sober and much celebrated 128 year old English football club – a globally recognised sporting 'brand' – briefly hung in the balance.'

The spectre of relegation was shockingly tangible. With the Reds already looking like they were stuck in the quagmire of a footballing dogfight to escape the dreaded drop, a deduction of nine points may well have been fatal – despite the redemptive football that was to come after Christmas. Less than eighteen months after the club had narrowly lost out on their first Premier League title, their place amongst the English elite – indeed, their very existence - was under threat.

On 13th October 2010, with supporters' nerves jangling and to a soundtrack of ever more vociferous demonstrating, Mr Justice Floyd gave a withering and damning assessment of the carry-on of the American cowboys, claiming they had been guilty of 'the clearest possible breach' of a corporate governance agreement and that it would be 'entirely wrong' to grant a counter claim to postpone the proposed sale of the club to NESV for £300 million. Though this was not the end of the case – the Americans would appeal in Texas and then be accused by Judge Floyd of having 'misled' their lawyers in the US – it effectively meant that Broughton and the board were free to go ahead with the sale to NESV. John Henry attended the board meeting that night and tweeted:

'Well done Martin, Christian and Ian. Well done RBS. Well done supporters!'

As he was serenaded by renditions of You'll Never Walk Alone from joyous supporters outside the court, Christian Purslow said he hoped the next decade would see 'calm and football being the story and business not being the story.'

Martin Broughton claimed that:

'We've been here to complete a sale process. We said at the outset that we'd find the right owners for Liverpool, I think we've done that. At the end, we had two viable bids, both of whom would have been the right owners. We had to choose between them and I think Liverpool Football Club can look forward to a bright future.'

Spirit of Shankly gave voice to the overall frustration of the fanbase and their anger at what the club had been put through under the hated regime (and, indeed, the mistakes of the previous owners):

'It's a victory, but it's a hollow victory. We shouldn't have been in this situation in the first place. The previous owners put us in this position and the current owners made it even worse. We are starting afresh now, but a club like Liverpool shouldn't be in this situation.'

This nearly terminal illness at the heart of the club, this putrefaction, which had threatened to reach out its tendrils and infect all aspects of our beloved Liverpool, had been excised and, even if there was still some questioning of the new owners and their intentions, results suddenly improved. It was as if the palpable gloom had been lifted and, for a short while, even Hodgson looked more comfortable in a dugout that had never seemed like a proper fit.

Let's be clear: redemption for Roy was never likely and the football was still less than sparkling, but after the horror show of the back-to-back losses to Blackpool and Everton, Liverpool seemed to find their groove to a degree and churned out some decent results. In late October and early November, the Reds won four games in a row, including an impressive 2-0 home win against Chelsea, during which Fernando Torres briefly threatened to rediscover his mojo. Alas, the inconsistency which had blighted the Reds' campaign soon returned with a vengeance at Wigan and Stoke before they were systematically outplayed by Tottenham, themselves – along with newly minted Manchester City – having now overtaken Liverpool in the long-term merciless fight for top four. Indeed, Champions League pretensions were very far from Kopites' minds as December became one of the worst months in recent history to be sitting in Anfield wearing a red shirt. A 3-1 capitulation at Newcastle United was followed up by another low point as Wolves, rooted to the foot of the table, visited a half empty Anfield and left with a fully deserved three points. For the first time in his tenure, the Liverpool manager heard his name echo through the terraces; it was, however, gallows Scouse humour as the cry went up again and again for 'Hodgson for England.' As the well-read and Kandinsky-loving Roy claimed that he was struggling for an adjective other than 'disappointing,' the downward sweep of the axe could be almost heard. There was a brief stay of execution following an anaemic 2-1 victory over Bolton Wanderers before the Liverpool manager was finally put out of his misery after an insipid and dismal 3-1 defeat away to Blackburn Rovers. The away end continued their championing of Hodgson's credentials as England manager (the irony!), while also very vocally pining for Dalglish as the home support gleefully asked could Blackburn play us every week while also enquiring 'were we Burnley in disguise?' In a season of rock-bottoms during a tortuous reign, this was yet another, but this time one there would be no recovery from.

NESV – now rebranded Fenway Sports Group – looked on from Boston and decided that the time had come to act. It would take a near mythical figure, an almost god-like being who had achieved legendary status at Liverpool, to unite a deeply ruptured and fractious fan base. Kenny Dalglish answered the call, and twenty years after walking away from his beloved Liverpool, returned from holiday early to take the reins of a club which was now very different from the one he had left behind.

The epithets (and, indeed epitaphs) that were laid at Hodgson's feet as he, apparently, left the club by mutual consent were, to Liverpool supporters, sickening and it would take nearly six years for the footballing world outside Merseyside to wake up to the myths surrounding the man. Yes, he was a capable manager – at a certain level – but was never a fit for Liverpool and his particular brand of defeatism rankled with Kopites. The media was full of crass and cringeworthy nods to 'a good footballing man' who had been harshly treated by a support which was mired in the past and had no appreciation of just how far their club had fallen.

This was, of course, utter nonsense; a large majority of Liverpool fans knew the landscape we were now competing in, knew how far the goalposts had been shifted. Practical financial doping at City and Chelsea had transformed the tapestry massively and, though there were some sections of our support who harboured ridiculously optimistic expectations, a large swathe of our fans understood the harsh realities facing Liverpool Football Club in this new modern arena. The problem with Hodgson had been his utter embracing of mediocrity, his soundbites and interviews which seemed designed to suck motivation from his players and the support, his ingratiating himself to rival managers, his complete failure to grasp what it meant to manage a club of the size and stature of Liverpool. The football was turgid, uninspiring, thoroughly lacking in ambition. Liverpool fans demanded more and it was all too easy to imagine a future where the club could become a ghastly echo of another northern giant, Newcastle United for example, one where fans were frequently bereft of hope. To be clear though, most Kopites never demanded the league title; they just demanded that it was never an impossibility; that there was some chance – however remote – that we could compete against the financial behemoths. Despite what the likes of Henry Winter – who, at this stage was waging a campaign to see Hodgson garner respect – wrote, the Reds had, after all, finished second in the league only eighteen months prior to Roy's calamitous reign. They had been the scourge of European heavyweights under Hodgson's predecessor and had been UEFA's top ranked side throughout the continent.

No, we didn't think we had a God-given right to success. But we deserved hope. Ultimately, that was the most damning indictment of Roy's time in charge. His tenure – along with the hated regime of Hicks and Gillett – was a graveyard to positive thoughts, a black hole to optimism.

But it felt like a new start as we woke up to the news that the King was returning. As Kenny's infectious smile lit up the travelling supports' mood when he waved to them at Old Trafford, it was as if hope had been reborn.

CHAPTER 18 - THE RETURN OF THE KING

Of course, nothing would be ever easy at Liverpool and, even if the appointment of Kenny Dalglish as interim manager had the vast majority of supporters in buoyant mood, the returning icon would have some severe issues to deal with.

Not least of these was a disgruntled Fernando Torres. Promises had been made to the Spanish striker and then broken – at least that was Torres' interpretation. There were strong rumours that he had been asked to play through his own personal pain barrier on a number of occasions and he had been left severely disillusioned at the direction the club had been sailing in following the ill-fated appointment of Hodgson. He was, however, far from alone in that.

Torres had gone from one of the best strikers in world football in his first few years with the club to a poor imitation of the golden-haired Achilles that had terrorised the best defences in European football. Liverpool supporters asked was it symptomatic of the general despondency that had engulfed the club or was it a sign of something more fundamental? Had injuries taken their toll on the striker and could he ever recapture the lightning pace and awe-inspiring assertiveness that made him such a formidable forward? Answers were not immediately apparent but even as the club heaved itself from the mire of disaffection and borderline apathy, with Dalglish walking back into Anfield, it rapidly became clear that Torres had had enough. The Spaniard had fallen out of love with the club or – at the very least – had ceased to love to play in a red shirt. Kenny's entreaties fell on apparent deaf ears; El Niño was determined to leave.

Nearly a year ago, Simon Hughes released his new book *Ring of Fire*, during which he interviewed Fernando Torres. This allowed the former striker to get some old grievances off his chest and to highlight his thinking in wanting to leave in early 2011; the truth is, it may have brought him desired trophies but he would never recapture the form that made him one of the best forwards in world football.

Newly appointed Director of Football, Damien Comolli, had originally envisioned the next arrival (during what suddenly became a frenetic January window) not as a replacement for the departing Spaniard but as one who would partner him in a saliva-inducing potential attack. Luis Suárez was signed from AFC Ajax; appearing to carry more baggage than an eighteenth century Saharan camel (and quite possibly the only reason Liverpool could get him for such a relatively modest fee), the Uruguayan may have possessed a questionable temperament but also doubtlessly possessed unique gifts. During a whirlwind three years at the club, all of these facets of this exceptional and inimitable footballer would be on stark display.

Less successful was arguably one of the most bizarre transfers in the club's history - although, when taken in tandem with the price of Torres, it definitely becomes less head-scratching - as Andy Carroll arrived from Newcastle United for the eye-popping fee of £35 million. New owners FSG, evidently determined to make a statement and prove that they were different from their predecessors, had apparently sanctioned a fee that was £15 million less than that received for Liverpool's departing number nine. In one way it was thrilling; a potential tricky attacker in Suárez teaming up with the proverbial 'big man with a good touch' and proof that our new owners were willing to invest. In another way it was troubling and bordering on myopic – like so many Liverpool transfers since the formation of the Premier League – as we acquired an injured striker in Carroll who had played a few months at the highest level and about whom rumours were already rife concerning his enjoyment of the high life. A spiky and intransigent Dalglish answered those who questioned the wisdom of the purchase by explaining the fee had been paid for the long term; ironic, then, that arguably Carroll's finest displays in the red of Liverpool would come near the end of his first injury ravaged season. As will be covered below, the Liverpool manager's transfer policy in the following summer appeared designed almost exclusively to get the most from his towering striker; it rarely worked and added to the pressure on the Scot and Comolli.

But as Dalglish basked in the adulation of a suddenly united Liverpool support, pressure was the least thing anyone would associate with the new tenure. Sure, there is a unique burden in managing Liverpool Football Club, but despite some early losses, Kenny seemed to be merely picking up where he had left off all those years ago. On 6th February, with marvellous serendipity, the Reds went to Stamford Bridge to face Torres' new employers – days after the Spaniard had signed for the Blues. A superbly taken Raul Meireles goal (with curious irony, one of the few successes of Hodgson but who only had months of his Liverpool career left) gave Dalglish's new charges a resounding victory and few will forget the celebration of the interim boss as El Niño looked on in stoic resignation. There were many more highlights to come as winter approached spring and a spring became evident in all of our steps. Manchester United – on course to win yet another Premier League title – were crushed 3-1 at Anfield as a beaming Kenny grinned in the sun in front of his adoring Kop. It was also a game where Suárez firmly announced himself to Liverpool – and indeed the league's – fans as he danced and tormented the United rearguard for ninety thrilling minutes and handed Dirk Kuyt the easiest hat-trick the Dutchman has ever scored in professional football. United's 'noisy neighbours' – now a bona fide Champions League-chasing side – were also dismantled shortly after as a returning Andy Carroll showed his physical gifts with a soaring header and a fierce left footed drive. In the next four games – two away and two at home – the Reds clocked up fourteen goals; a 1-1 draw with Arsenal in which Kuyt, much to Arsène Wenger's ire (and Kenny's elation) scored an equalising penalty in the 97th minute; a 5-0 victory over Birmingham City in which Maxi Rodriguez scored a deftly executed finish (and even Joe Cole roused himself from his apparent somnambulism in red to notch a goal); a terrific 3-0 defeat of Newcastle and a 5-2 obliteration of Fulham, during which Maxi plundered another three goals. Following the latter result, Liverpool, who had seemed to be stuck in a relegation quagmire only a few months before, now found themselves in fifth place and with an outside chance of Champions League qualification. It was a quite stunning turnaround and even subsequent defeats in the final two games of the season could not rob Kopites of a huge feeling of hopefulness as the season ended. With a wave of euphoria washing over them even as far as Boston from the Liverpool fans, FSG effectively had little choice; possibly against their initial feelings, Kenny Dalglish was handed the role of Liverpool manager on a full time basis. Few would, or could, argue at the time that it was not the right appointment.

Kenny's success as he had taken the reins at a troubled club had been built around the talented and mentally quick Maxi, Meireles and Suárez, with the likes of Kuyt offering excellent support. But with his first season as manager proper dawning, Dalglish and his director of football essentially tore up this blueprint and decided to start from scratch. This was, to a degree, understandable; as Andy Carroll – the club's record purchase – strained at the leash to prove he was fit and firing, his manager sought to bring in personnel who would get the best from the Geordie. Moreover, Maxi was not getting any younger and, clearly, Meireles was not entirely trusted. It could be argued, however, that it was yet another example of the Reds seeking to change too much, too soon and dispensing with effective weapons prematurely. Certainly the players identified by Dalglish and Comolli – with one exception – would never really convince in a red shirt. FSG were determined to spend big and spend they did, but it could be argued that the signings were a touch simplistic and showed just how long Dalglish had been out of the game. Stuart Downing arrived from Aston Villa for just over £18 million; fresh from a season in which he had been the Villains' player of the year, it was envisaged that he would supply the bullets for Carroll. Alas, the Liver bird never sat comfortably on the English winger's chest. Talented though he was, it was a classic case of the shirt being too heavy. This charge would also be initially laid at the feet of another big money Englishman to arrive as many questioned the wisdom of handing Sunderland £16 million for the unproven midfielder Jordan Henderson. Though his initial seasons would underwhelm as he was played out of position, dropped and genuinely seemed to struggle with expectation, the Teessider would ultimately prove good value and a shrewd buy. The same could not be said of José Enrique, a left-back signed from Newcastle for £6 million, whose Liverpool career, like the painting of Dorian Gray, went in the polar opposite of Henderson's; initially exciting but rapidly showing his limitations. In yet another ploy to harness Carroll's undoubted ability – in the right system – Charlie Adam was brought in from relegated Blackpool. The Scot had superb ability from a dead ball but little in the way of brains, grace or footballing intelligence; he would last only as long as the manager who signed him.

A raft of first teamers were shown the door by Dalglish with those players who appeared to sum up the recent plights of the Reds ushered out - – whether fairly or not – including Konchesky, Milan Jovanovic, Kyrgiakos, Poulsen and N'Gog. Perhaps most surprising was the transfer of Raul Meireles to Chelsea for £12 million on the final day of the 2011's summer transfer window. As mentioned, he had appeared the one real bright spark of all Hodgson's inept dealings in the market and had displayed a keen eye for goal and clever, incisive movement since December. Perhaps it was he was just never truly suited to English football (as evidenced by his future career). Or perhaps his constantly bewildering haircuts upset his phlegmatic and staid manager.

Regardless, many pundits viewed the Reds as genuine dark horses in the race for the top four. Without European football and with a manager who had finally united the fan base, it was just possible that Liverpool could see off the challenges of the new pretenders Spurs and Man City and that of the old guard, the daunting troika of Manchester United, Arsenal and Chelsea. Certainly the start made by the Reds to the 2011/12 campaign did little to dampen the flames of tentative expectation. Sunderland may have held the Reds to a disappointing opening day draw at Anfield but Liverpool's support were soon bouncing again with a 2-0 victory at the

Emirates over Arsenal and an effusive 3-1 hammering of Bolton Wanderers, during which Suárez continued to dazzle and display his nascent genius. Unfortunately, an utterly inept display in September against Spurs resulted in a 4-0 defeat; the brilliance of Luka Modric pulling the strings and the predatory instincts of Adebayor and Defoe highlighting the job that Kenny actually had on his hands in restoring the club to something approaching how he had left it. However, Liverpool rallied and then went on a long unbeaten run which wouldn't end until early December when a Clint Dempsey late strike gave Fulham victory. During this run, there was an infamous encounter with Manchester United; despite an innocuous enough 1-1 draw, the game became notorious for allegations of racism from Luis Suárez towards the United left-back, Patrice Evra, and subsequently the Uruguayan being found guilty and handed an eight match ban (more of this – and the role played by Liverpool Football Club – will be discussed in the next part of the book).

Despite the Fulham setback, the Reds were handily placed for an assault on the top four and two victories and two draws in the remaining games of the year saw Liverpool in fifth, level on points with fourth placed Chelsea. Progress had also been made in the League Cup, most notably a 2-0 victory over Chelsea at Stamford Bridge, a 2-1 away defeat of Stoke City (with an early goal of the season contender in Suárez's thrilling, bending winner) and a 5-1 obliteration of Oldham Athletic. As the festive season gave way to January, there was plenty of cause for positivity with Liverpool handily placed in the league and with a League Cup Semi-Final against Manchester City to look forward to.

CHAPTER 19 TURMOIL AND CUP FINALS

It was as if the match – and the resulting fracas – cast a belligerent curse on the football club and the remainder of the season.

Two weeks after the Reds had knocked Manchester United out of the FA Cup, the great northern rivals met again in the league at Old Trafford in what was Luis Suárez's return from suspension, after being found guilty of racially abusing Patrice Evra. After the Uruguayan decided not to shake Evra's hand, the contest itself almost became an afterthought. *The Times* put it succinctly:

That a game – and a result – of such significance as far as the championship is concerned could get quite so lost amid the rancour and recriminations that flowed in the wake of Suárez's refusal to shake Evra's hand served to underline just how raw a nerve this sorry saga has touched. Match of the Day felt inclined to show three replays of the handshake that never was but not one of any of the three goals … '

Luis Suárez was now firmly cast as the pantomime villain of English football.

It was in October, during what initially appeared to be a fairly insignificant incident, that the die had originally been cast. This is not a commentary on the legal status of the FA's verdict, or the veracity of the case brought against the Liverpool striker. He was found guilty, fined £40,000 and banned for eight games. To this day, Suárez pleads his innocence and, in his recent autobiography, claimed that the incident placed 'a stain on my character that will probably be there forever.'

But the whole regretful situation also placed a strain on the manager.

There can be little doubt about it; Kenny Dalglish's interviews became more pugnacious as he bristled in front of the cameras. Always taciturn and reluctant with the media, the Scot, to a degree left on his own to deal with a mess not of his making, became palpably affected by having to deal with issues unrelated to football on a constant basis. The case itself was damaging to the club, the aftermath more damaging still. In Suárez's final game before he began his suspension, the players endeavoured to show solidarity with their team mate by wearing tee shirts with his image and name emblazoned on the front. It should be noted here that the verdict was never completely cut and dry and the official line from the club was that, even though they wished to 'stamp out racism in every form, inside and outside the club,' they had a 'strongly held conviction that the Football Association and the panel it selected constructed a highly subjective case … based on an accusation that was ultimately unsubstantiated.'

The players' unity with Suárez garnered widespread criticism; *The Guardian* claiming that 'this was a high profile international found guilty of racial abuse 24 hours earlier and they were inappropriate gestures at this stage of an already damaging saga.'

Speaking some months later, Dalglish claimed this had had nothing to do with his sacking:

'I think it was the club as a whole. It wasn't just me making decisions. The T-shirts were the players wanting to show their support for a team-mate. It might have been misguided and not have been right but it was not me that decided it.'

The whole episode may not have led directly to Kenny's sacking but the season was on the cusp of unravelling very publically. There were some poor results during Suárez's suspension (the nadir probably being an utterly abject 3-1 defeat to Bolton Wanderers) and by the time of the outcry over the Uruguayan's failure to shake hands, the Reds were sitting in seventh place in the Premier League. Dalglish, Ian Ayre and Suárez himself were all forced to issue apologies over the handling of the situation as a club who once proudly dealt with all problems with dignity now toyed again with negative headlines. When Arsenal visited Anfield and somehow left with a 2-1 win thanks to a gut-wrenching late goal from van Persie, any lingering hope of finishing in the top four was all but extinguished.

However, though league form would soon descend into almost Hodgsonesque levels of ineptitude, the cup runs were a not inconsiderable bright spot (and surely a mitigating factor for the Premier League travails). Liverpool stirringly beat Manchester City over two legs in the League Cup Semi-Final to set up a Wembley clash with Championship side Cardiff City (the Reds' first visit to what had once been called 'Anfield South' since 2006). The performance was not a vintage one as Liverpool laboured to a 2-2 draw but eventually prevailed on penalties, though few Kopites were not moved by an emotional Kenny Dalglish, tear strewn as victory was confirmed, as he finally captured some silverware for his beloved Liverpool.

The FA Cup exploits would not have quite the same dénouement, despite some epics all the way to the final. Oldham Athletic had been crushed 5-1 in the third round before the aforementioned 2-1 victory over Manchester United. A memorable semi-final with Everton was decided by a late Andy Carroll goal as the Geordie's late season form briefly gave Liverpool fans hope that he could be a genuine success. The final against Chelsea, however, was another dispiriting apotheosis of anti-climactic as the Reds never really got going until the introduction of Carroll at which stage they had found themselves 2-0 down. A few minutes after his introduction, the former Newcastle striker halved the deficit and, but for a frankly logic-defying save from Petr Cech, would have sent the game into extra time. But overall the game was Liverpool's season in a nutshell; disappointing and too little, too late.

As Liverpool limped to the league finishing line and eighth place in the table with a weak and utterly forgettable 1-0 defeat by Swansea City, Dalglish was hearing reports that the Wigan manager, Roberto Martínez, was favourite for his job. Damian Comolli and head of sports science Peter Brukner had already been axed as FSG started to show their ruthlessness and intolerance for any kind of failure. Dalglish, despite recording the club's joint worst league finish since before Shankly took over and overseeing fourteen Premier League defeats, was defiant after the latest disappointing result.

"I would expect the owners to have more dignity and integrity than to believe a story in the newspapers," said the Scot. *"We'll not run away from the points tally, we'll face up to reality."*

Nevertheless, a few days later, on 16th May, Dalglish was summoned to Boston and sacked. It must have been an extremely difficult time for him but Kenny was – as always – the very definition of dignified respect:

I am disappointed with results in the league, but I would not have swapped the Carling Cup win for anything as I know how much it meant to our fans and the club to be back winning trophies. It has been an honour and a privilege to have had a chance to come back as the Liverpool manager. Whilst I am obviously disappointed to be leaving, the matter has been handled by the owners and all concerned in an honourable, respectful and dignified way and reflects the quality of the people involved and their continued desire to move the football club forward.'

John Henry was rightfully lavish in his praise for a genuine Liverpool icon:

'Kenny will always be more than a championship winning manager, more than a championship winning player. He is in many ways the heart and soul of the club. He personifies everything that is good about Liverpool Football Club. He has always put the club and its supporters first. Kenny will always be a part of the family at Anfield.'

Few would argue with this assessment but Dalglish returned to a very different game than the one he had left a decade previous. Football had evolved rapidly and massively in a few short years and he spent £120 million essentially trying to get the best from a target man. That statement may be bordering on jejune and doing Kenny a disservice but, at the very least, there were whisperings that many of the first team – even if they had nothing but admiration for the Scot – had misgivings about his tactical nous. Thirty seven points behind the new Premier League champions, Manchester City, and seventeen points adrift of fourth placed Spurs – a club with a lower budget and wage bill – meant Dalglish was always going to be under pressure ('We'd be disappointed if we're not in the top four,' Henry had stated before a ball had been kicked). But Kenny left as he had arrived in January 2010; with his head held high and with the respect of the entire fan base (one he had virtually single-handedly united) for all he had done for his club.

Former manager Rafa Benítez and Roberto Martínez were the media's immediate front runners to replace Kenny Dalglish with the Germans Joachim Löw and Jürgen Klopp apparently also in the frame. But it was an Ulsterman, the up and coming Swansea City manager Brendan Rodgers (who had, ironically, inflicted Kenny's last ever defeat) who FSG turned to in order to convert their footballing blueprint into a reality. A 180-page manifesto, in which Rodgers highlighted his philosophy and how he planned to win football matches, impressed the club's owners at his initial interview and all but guaranteed him the job. He was unveiled as the new manager on the 1st June 2012.

Among the Liverpool fan base, some were underwhelmed and some were scornful because Rodgers had won nothing and was not Kenny. A considerable part of the support were, however, prepared to give him a chance – particularly after a highly impressive first press conference. The former Swansea manager certainly talked the talk; but walking the walk would be more difficult, and most fans anticipated yet another transitional season. Rodgers turned to two players he had coached before as his first signings: the diminutive pair of Joe Allen and Fabio Borini for a combined fee of just over £25 million. Oussama Assaidi and Samed Yesil also arrived as the first murmurs of the transfer committee (two words that would soon acquire proper noun status) started to enter the Anfield lexicon. There were also some notable departures with Dirk Kuyt, Maxi Rodríguez, Alberto Aquilani, Craig Bellamy, Charlie Adam and Joe Cole (loan) all leaving the club. Finally, Nuri Sahin arrived on a loan from Real Madrid in a deal that initially appeared to be something of a coup. The talented Turk would, however, only last a few months. Rodgers also tried to offload Jordan Henderson to Fulham in exchange for Clint Dempsey but the young midfielder dug his heels in and showed the tenacity that he would soon begin to display on a football pitch. That shambolic transfer deadline day still sends shivers of disgust down the spine of many Liverpool fans as the club failed to sign a striker to replace Andy Carroll, who Rodgers clearly didn't want and who was sent on loan to West Ham. As the 2012/13 season began, the Reds had one senior fit striker in Luis Suárez.

Rodgers' new charges began encouragingly enough with a 4-0 aggregate win over Gomel in the Europa League's (the rebranded UEFA Cup) qualifying round. But the manager soon had a chance to view the Herculean task he had inherited when Liverpool were beaten 3-0 by West Brom on the opening day of the campaign. Though the next match against the champions was a highly promising 2-2 draw, the Reds wouldn't win a league game until the end of September when Suárez started what would become a bi-annual torture of Norwich City in a 5-2 victory. Raheem Sterling, the precocious teenager signed by Benítez towards the end of the Spaniard's reign, was blooded in these early games and looked a terrific prospect as he opened his account against Reading in a 1-0 victory.

But in those games before Christmas – both domestically and in Europe – consistency remained tantalisingly out of reach. After an encouraging run of wins in early December (a run that had Rodgers talking loftily of challenging for second place), Aston Villa visited Anfield and departed with a 3-1 win. The Reds then took Fulham apart in a 4-0 victory, only to be utterly limp and flaccid in losing 3-1 to Stoke City on Boxing Day, four days later. As 2012 became 2013, Liverpool were in tenth place in the league, twenty one points behind the leaders, Manchester United.

But though we couldn't possibly have foreseen it then, two new signings, along with a rapidly crystallising world class talent in Luis Suárez, were about to help propel the Reds to practically unimaginable heights.

CHAPTER 20 - POETRY IN MOTION

It wouldn't be too much of a stretch to suggest that there was something of a collective shrug of scouse shoulders as Brendan Rodgers and the transfer committee secured the signings of Daniel Sturridge and Philippe Coutinho. Both were the very epitome of the FSG, Moneyball-inspired blueprint; ultra-talented and young but not quite hitting the heights that their respective talents suggested they were capable of. Though there was the inevitable residual excitement that comes with any transfer of a mercurial South American, there was also a healthy dose of grounded realism – the £8.5 million arrival from Inter Milan had hardly set the world alight during his time in Italy, although a loan spell at RCD Espanyol pointed to a ceiling, in terms of talent, that could be very high indeed.

The English international striker Sturridge was, patently unfairly, seen by many as possessing a mercenary streak and a player that may have been difficult to work with though, it has to be noted, much of the unease stemmed from the fact that many Kopites were also uncomfortable about the Reds signing footballers that were essentially cast-offs from their perceived rivals. But the reality was that Roman Abramovich's insistence on big names at Chelsea worked in Liverpool's favour; Sturridge would soon usurp Fernando Torres as one of the best strikers in the Premier League and would do so in a red shirt. Even the most unbridled of optimists would be hard-pressed to have predicted it in January of 2013, but the arrival of an Englishman and a Brazilian was about to provide the catalyst for what would be a thrilling eighteen months.

In Brendan Rodgers' first few months at the club, there had been a perception that his stunningly gifted striker, Luis Suárez, had tried to do too much on his own, possibly not trusting the level of talent that was around him in the Liverpool attack. But the Uruguayan instantly recognised the potential of the new arrivals and this thrillingly effective triumvirate would serve up some sumptuous football over the coming spring, an electrifying and exhilarating appetizer for the main course Liverpool fans were about to dine on in 2013/14. In his autobiography, *Crossing the Line*, Suárez described his impression of his new teammates:

'Philippe was incredible. He changed us completely. He's the one that gave us faith in having the ball because his technical ability is so good. You knew that he wouldn't lose it, you knew that he would produce something special … you could see straight away that he was different. Daniel was about to become the best partner I'd had in my career … I could see that he would make a difference. When I watched him in training, my appreciation for his ability grew. I knew that he was quick but the way that he could finish really struck me. Every shot went in. Every time. He had the talent and Liverpool offered him the opportunity and continuity that he hadn't had at Chelsea.'

This new-look attacking force would immediately start to sow the seeds that would fully flower in the following season as they routinely put teams to the sword and racked up impressive wins in the second half of the 12/13 campaign. Norwich City were trounced 5-0 in a game that was notable for Suárez, the chief canary tormentor, only scoring one goal and Sturridge becoming the first Liverpool player since Ray Kennedy to find the net in his first three competitive games for the club. Suárez may have only notched the one against his favourite victims but he was in the middle of a prolific season as his astonishing gifts were rapidly solidifying. A hat-trick against Wigan Athletic in a 4-0 victory graphically demonstrated the Uruguayan's goal scoring prowess but his past indiscretions were undermining his chances of securing a PFA or Football Writer's award for player of the season. As *The Times* put it:

'Of the three leading contenders for the PFA award, Van Persie and Gareth Bale being the other two, Suarez's performance indicators have been the most eye-catching. Not only has he now scored more goals than his two rivals and has a superior goals-to-minute ratio, he also has more assists, made more key passes and more tackles. This in a Liverpool side in which he has been the only available recognised forward for a large period of time.'

Alas, as the season entered its final few games, the divisive Suárez handed the moral high ground to his detractors and sealed himself as the practically unrivalled pantomime villain of English football as he, quite shamefully, decided to bite Chelsea's Branislav Ivanovic during the dying moments of a 2-2 draw at Anfield.

But ….

Well this is too forensic; too dispassionate. Poetry, outside of an English literature class, is rarely pathological. Who wants to study the mechanics of iambic pentameter or onomatopoeia when you can savour *Ozymandias* or *Mid-term Break* or *Paradise Lost*? We all know what happened to our Uruguayan striker, we all know the package that Suárez came wrapped in, a flawed hero that was about to explode in a kaleidoscopic burst of redemption as his unique talent crystallised, as his journey towards the very elite players in world football took a beguiling and thrilling quantum leap. To return to the poetical metaphor, and at the risk of stretching it too far, for Suárez and his cohorts that were about to thrill a new generation of Reds, it was Milton's *Paradise Regained*.

First though, with Suárez in the midst of a ban for his latest misdemeanour, and during an underwhelming summer of transfer dealings as, one after another, targets slipped through Red fingers, Brendan Rodgers had to fight off interest from Arsenal for the Reds' talismanic striker. The Gunners submitted a transfer bid which elicited the now-famous tweet from John Henry as he speculated on the possible narcotic preferences of the London club's hierarchy. Whatever they were indeed smoking at the Emirates, there was no whiff of indecision from the Liverpool manager as he summarily banished Suárez, now agitating for a move, to train with the reserves as he served out the remainder of his suspension.

Looking back, it's easy to wonder what could have been had the Reds secured even one of their top transfer targets during the summer of 2013. Henrikh Mkhitaryan, Willian and Diego Costa were all pursued by Rodgers but in the end the Reds' boss had to settle for Luis Alberto, Iago Aspas and Victor Moses (the latter on loan from Chelsea). Could one of the former trio have made a difference as the roaring flames of the 2013/14 post-Christmas form became less brilliant and deafening as the spring became summer. A lack of squad rotation and Rodgers' distrust of anyone outside of a cadre of around thirteen players, have all been mooted as possible reasons for Liverpool's thrilling challenge eventually fading. But then would a Willian or Mkhitaryan (Costa was almost surely never a realistic prospect as he angled for one final release clause caveated contract from Atlético Madrid) have held back the exhilarating and electrifying development of Raheem Sterling who, from November onwards, was one of the finest young players in Europe? We will never know the answer but the chemistry that was gradually built by Rodgers, the breathtaking interaction between the forward line as side after side toppled and were utterly vanquished, quite probably would not have fermented so well if one of the aforementioned trio had signed.

But, again, this is bordering on the forensic. Screw that.

The campaign that would develop into a mass, collective deluge of singing from the stands, of 'We are Liverpool' cascading throughout Anfield as goals and goals and more goals were witnessed with feverish joy, began – not with a bang – but with a series of relatively formulaic (but highly encouraging) wins. But is it memory playing tricks on me as I peer back in my mind? Is it viewing the beginning of the season through a prism of Red optimism that was to later unfurl if I claim on August 17th, when new goalkeeper Simon Mignolet dived to his right to keep out Jonathan Walters' last minute penalty and deny Stoke City a share of the spoils, that there was a faint stirring of nascent belief? Belief that we may be on the cusp of something special, that Liverpool were quite possibly in the midst of the planets aligning themselves perfectly in our favour (let's not mention storms; even if they are of the 'perfect variety'. The very phrase irks at this stage).

Ferguson's phenomenal regime was at an end up the road in Manchester and there was more than a hint that it was, in reality, the sheer force of his personality that that had dragged Manchester United to their twentieth league title. The Red Devils' noisy neighbours, a year after Sergio Agüero's dramatic last gasp winner had given them their first Premier League title, had parted company with Roberto Mancini and there were many who speculated that it may take his successor, the Chilean Manuel Pellegrini, a while to adjust to the unique rigours of the English Premier League. Chelsea had reappointed José Mourinho and he himself wrote off his new charge's chances relatively early with his frankly ridiculous comparison to 'little ponies'. Why should Liverpool think they should be discussed in comparative terms with these sides when, for the last few seasons, our rivals had, in reality, been more mid-table sides then the traditional table toppers? Because – and this is not hindsight talking – the belief already discussed had been slowly coursing through Red veins, building from a trickle to a surge, as the form at the end of the previous season had been cause for vast encouragement. It only took Mignolet's save and three successive winners from Daniel Sturridge – truly stepping up in the absence of Suárez – to help this surge become a tide, a sparkling Red sea of hope and anticipation.

Late September witnessed the return of Suárez (now, apparently, rehabilitated and ready to give his all) with Liverpool handily placed, despite a hugely disappointing home defeat to Southampton which had, for many, confirmed that we could still not quite trust these Reds. We all knew the Uruguayan was special, but he was about to show us just how unique a player Liverpool possessed. Arguably, from October through until February, there was no finer player plying their trade anywhere on the planet. It was astonishing, almost surreal, as Suárez seemed to be playing his own personal goal of the season competition. Who will forget his impromptu, improbable header from outside the box against West Brom or the fabulously cheeky nutmeg and outside-of-the-foot finish that preceded it? Or what about the finest example of finishing I have ever witnessed in one game as Suárez absolutely tormented Norwich City in early December. We watched something truly special, truly enchanting, that crisply chilly evening at Anfield and, if you'll forgive me an indulgence, I have to re-create part of an article that I wrote for the *The Tomkins Times* website not long after:

Anfield, 3rd December, 2013. Pre-Christmas cheer, the stadium feels slightly devoid of passion, there is a troubling disquiet in the air. We have been to Hull and back, have been handed our arses on a plate and have retreated meekly following an abjectly laboured and dull display. The media are already doom-mongering, pointing to portents that our Champions League push will, typically and inevitably, shrivel and die before the festive season begins. Liverpool have not begun this game against Norwich City particularly well; their passing game is slightly off and Norwich are having some joy with their high pressing. And then Luis Suárez, quite literally out of nowhere, transforms and transcends the mood. His is a forty-five yard volley of miraculous intent; an arc of triumph that gloriously soars, dipping and swerving, from his foot over a hapless Ruddy in the Norwich City goal. Ten minutes later the Uruguayan actually betters his brilliant first with a goal of such quality, cheek and imagination that it really defies description. And just for good measure during this astonishing performance, Suárez also indulges us with a fabulously improvised finish and an expertly-taken thirty yard free kick. Has there ever been a show of such breathtaking finishing witnessed at Anfield in all its illustrious history? Is there another footballer on the planet that could produce such a range of goals? Probably not and this performance completely and utterly obliterates any talk of throwing in the Champions League towel.

In the space of a week, just before we collectively sat down for our Yuletide dinners with the Reds gloriously looking down from the summit of the Premier League, Suárez destroyed Cardiff City almost single-handedly, one of his goals a ridiculously bending, curling, piece of artistry as he showed his vast intelligence, skill and appreciation for angles, while he also played a massive part in Liverpool's dismantling of Spurs at White Hart Lane. The latter was, thus far, the zenith of Rodgers' Reds as they, shorn of Steven Gerrard and Daniel Sturridge, summarily dismantled André Villas-Boas' Tottenham side. The dismayed, stricken and defeated manager simply became the first of a few to be sacked following obliteration by a Red tsunami. Former Spurs boss David Pleat opined that '(it) was a masterclass, a display of exhilarating football. Liverpool were speedy and purposeful with brilliant individual touches. They have produced a superb away performance.' The injured captain Gerrard sat in the Sky Sports studio, and as he waxed lyrical about the Reds, he may have been forgiven for wondering if his undeniably aging legs could again find a place in this dynamic and lethal outfit.

Stevie also sat out the next two games as Liverpool – dauntingly – faced both Manchester City and Chelsea away in the space of three days. The Reds were unfortunate in the extreme to emerge with no points from the brace of fixtures but the display at the Etihad Stadium in particular had Kopites purring and wondering just what could be achieved this season. But these losses saw Liverpool plummet to fifth in the league in what was starting to become a very congested top six.

The conundrum facing Rodgers – how best to get the captain back in the side – did not appear to be solved as Aston Villa came to Anfield in mid-January and raced into a 2-0 lead. Gerrard was deployed in a holding midfield role, part quarter back, part regista, in a bold move by Rodgers, and one that has been, to a degree, airbrushed in a flurry of revisionism since. Though the Reds fought back to secure a draw, many questioned the decision. It would prove to be a master stroke as Stevie got used to the position; all of his still formidable gifts, his ability to launch missiles, his razor-sharp footballing brain, and the sheer range to his passing were all to the fore as the season started to enter a critical stage. Gerrard may have not been able to quite get around the field like the captain of old, but in a rapidly maturing Jordan Henderson, Liverpool had an indefatigable Duracell bunny who could compensate for his captain's relative lack of mobility.

By the end of January, as Liverpool welcomed their neighbours from across Stanley Park to Anfield, there was no sense that we were about to embark on a near-historic run of results. Though the Reds were hopeful of securing a place in the top four and a return to the Promised Land of Champions League football, this was by no means certain. Everton, under Roberto Martínez, were on an upward trajectory and sat a mere two points behind Liverpool in fifth with a game in hand. Tottenham Hotspur were also breathing down our necks and, though they were hilariously floundering under the leadership of 'The Chosen One' David Moyes, Manchester United could never be discounted (at least at this stage of that season). Gerrard again started the Merseyside derby at the base of the midfield and there was a sense of slight trepidation as the teams walked out under the winter floodlights. Four goals later and all fears were forgotten – if not quite banished, then certainly brushed under the carpet as Liverpool fans gloried in another masterclass. But still, despite the nature of the win, despite the joy we got from Sturridge's lob and Gerrard's header and Suárez's run and adroit finish, there remained a lingering, inherent doubt. It had been a fine season so far but third was probably the best we could hope for. Slight distrust continued to loiter in the stands of Anfield and elsewhere. These barely articulated fears, that this campaign could still go pear-shaped, were merely given some credence by the following result, a disappointing 1-1 draw with West Brom.

Where were you at 12.30 on Saturday 8th February 2014? Can you picture your surroundings? Can you feel the air around you, the angst fuelled disquiet as the league leaders arrived at Anfield? Is it still there within you, persistent, enduring, that sense of incredulity as this fantastic tapestry unfolded before your eyes? The Spurs annihilation had been good but this was something more; this was a harbinger, a paean to glory scarcely felt, scarcely believed. This was all of our fears being dismantled as each goal went in, all of our hopes beginning to crystallise and swarm and gather a locomotive life of their own, a force that would not be denied and that would gather pace. Coutinho effervescent, robbing Mesut Özil, pressing like a rabid wolf, finding space, finding Sturridge. Said England striker's deadly, relentless, probing, exquisite touch. Suárez, the djinn, the force of nature and chaos, a Loki made flesh, tormenting the league leaders and scoring the best goal of the season that wasn't a goal as the inside of the post shuddered with the power of his talent. Henderson and Sterling, the great hopes, the transformation from sources of worry and irritable cynicism to stars being completed before our eyes, a benign metamorphosis in the space of a few months. Škrtel, the foundation of many a fear, the epicentre of unease for so long, continuing his unlikely goal scoring exploits.

5-1. And we never looked back. We refused to look back. We simply rolled our sleeves up and made the impossible dream a tantalising reality. Test after test came and were dealt with, hurdles were jumped. Dreams were forged.

But first the players had to believe. Personally, I feel that Gerrard's winning penalty a few days later against Fulham was when they started to consider the title a genuine possibility. Watch Stevie's leap as the Reds complete the comeback, watch as he strips off his jersey, as he clenches his arm in intoxicating and contagious triumph. This was not now about securing a top four place, not anymore; this was now about the title. About the Premier League.

It continued to rain goals. Goals from everywhere, goals from every angle. Suárez – after his phenomenal early to mid-season form – wasn't quite the impossible whirlwind he had been but others stepped up. Sterling became a new darling, Coutinho revelled and hinted at just what he could become capable of in the fullness of time, Sturridge just kept scoring until injury halted his inexorable feats. Twelve (12) goals scored in three consecutive away games against Southampton, Manchester United and Cardiff City signalled a virtual parade in the streets surrounding Anfield as Liverpool welcomed Sunderland with a giddy flood of red and smoke and sheer joy.

We all believed.

We believed when The Mackems – fighting desperately for their lives – were dismissed, despite some scares. We believed when Tottenham, now starting to buckle under Tim Sherwood, were swatted contemptuously aside at Anfield. We believed when two penalties from our captain foiled the pantomime villain that was Sam Allardyce and usurped his nefarious plans to neuter the claws of the Tricky Reds.

Anfield, 13th April, two days before the 25th anniversary of the

Hillsborough disaster. A sun-dappled pitch, a heaving throng of Red, a strident sea – no, ocean – of belief and pride. Brendan Rodgers, proud and determined, overlooks his troops, overlooks the stadium as 'You'll Never Walk Alone' is belted out, as voice after voice joins in, as flags wave and ripple in the gentle breeze. The very atmosphere seems to exclaim in a dissonant flourish: 'this is ours, this title is ours, it will not be taken from us.'

A win will put the dream in our hands – with only four league games left to play – for the first time.

The blitzkrieg is so typical of so much of the past season as Manchester City – league leaders and pre-kick-off favourites for the title – look shell-shocked. There is no spite in the booing and baying of the Anfield crowd whenever a blue shirt has the ball, there is no malevolence; there is only want, of need, of desire to see a sweet dénouement fulfilled, to see destiny writ large. Sterling's goal is a thing of beauty, a swaying, beguiling movement that bamboozles Vincent Kompany and Joe Hart. Sturridge and Gerrard should probably score as the cacophonous crowd roar their heroes on. Škrtel's glancing header makes it 2-0 and there is such an outpouring of release and of joy that it is hard to even write these words. That feeling is still there, still tangible.

But that feeling is about to get better.

Manchester City are league favourites for a reason; theirs is a formidable squad, full of skill and strength and bite. They fight back in the second half after some typically questionable Liverpool defending makes it 2-2. Minutes later, David Silva is the length of a boot's stud from connecting with Agüero's low cross and giving City the lead, with an open goal gaping.

Tension, palpable fear, bile rising in your throat, nerves shredded. And then the 78th minute, when Coutinho swivels following a Kompany miscue.

Then the eruption.

Then the last few minutes, of the previous fear and anguish made to seem like a picnic in Disneyland, of Hendo walking but us scarcely noticing. All eyes are on that clock, on the referee's whistle as time slows to a shrinking puddle in the spring sun.

If you are reading this now, you witnessed that. You witnessed that magic. You will never forget it and nor should you. Never forget the tears in the captain's eyes as he gathers his teammates in a circle and entreats them with a scouser's passion, in the hoarse voice of one who lost a family member twenty five years previously to an unimaginable catastrophe.

'This does not fucking slip.'

I have to blink away the tears as I write this. Harrowing, beyond cruel, what is to come. Let's not go there, let's leave it at the image of a tumultuous, triumphant Anfield, of banners and flags waving in glorious victory. Let's leave it with the image of the sun shining down from a clear blue sky that afternoon, when it all seemed – not just possible – but probable. The pain is too great to do anything else, is still a festering wound.

But, even with that haunting and devastating end, it was still poetry.

There's a cult film that was made in Ireland around the same time as when the Reds last won the league. *The Commitments*, a flick about a Dublin working class band trying to make it in the music industry and coming tantalisingly close to a breakthrough. One of the characters, with the memorable moniker of Joey 'the Lips' Fagan gives a practical Shakespearean soliloquy to the crestfallen band's manager towards the end of the movie:

'I know you're hurtin' now, but in time you'll realise what you achieved. You're missin' the point. The success of the band was irrelevant – you raised their expectations of life, you lifted their horizons. Sure we could have been famous and made albums and stuff, but that would have been predictable. This way it's poetry.'

And it was poetry.

Poetry in motion.

CHAPTER 21 - ANOTHER HANGOVER

Stewart Downing had just utterly negated the influence of Steven Gerrard on a football pitch.

Let that sink in. Downing, now a West Ham player after he had been shown the door by Rodgers at the start of the 13/14 season, had, barely a year later, gained some form of revenge.

3-1 to the Hammers on a cold Saturday evening towards the end of September and those heady, gorgeous days of late spring felt like an eternity away. This felt stifling, felt like a rancid morning after the night before, the memory of the revelry sickening as we tried to come to terms with the new reality. This felt all too familiar.

Liverpool had been here before, of course. Both previous times in the Premier League when the Reds had really looked like breaking their hoodoo and finally capturing that elusive trophy, the following season had been a grim swimming towards a new consciousness, a waking up to despair. Houllier had tasted a similar bitter vintage in 2003 as had Benítez in 2010. Brendan Rodgers made it a hat-trick of hangovers following the incredulity which became belief of the previous campaign. Though Rodgers could, like his predecessors, point to some mitigating circumstances that contributed to this season becoming such a desolate one, by the time this period had ended the Liverpool manager had lost the vast majority of fans.

To stretch a metaphor though, the last real party had been Norwich away in the early summer of 2014. By the time the Reds, almost visibly wilting and scarred following two harrowing matches against Chelsea and Crystal Palace, faced off against Newcastle United in the final game of the season, the coming hangover was, in hindsight, almost palpable. Liverpool's players had given everything, had ridden the crest of an emotional wave but had fallen at the final hurdle. They looked shattered as Newcastle took the lead on a Sunday afternoon, yet another definition of anticlimactic. That, thanks to two brilliant set piece assists (again) from Gerrard, Liverpool fought back to win their last game was testament to the team spirit that had been forged by Rodgers. But for the first time ever, there was a Premier League trophy at Anfield on the final day of the season; though unlikely, Man City could still throw the title away. That they never looked like slipping up and took an early lead merely compounded the empty feeling of loss, of coming so agonisingly close.

The comedown would be a merciless one indeed.

In the summer of 2014 however, there was still cause for cautious optimism. Though some fans had never taken to Brendan Rodgers, the majority were firmly behind him at this stage and the general feeling was that we had gotten our club back, that the Reds could consolidate and, if not win the title in the coming year, certainly secure another route back into the Champions League. Many hoped that Suárez may say no to Spanish super clubs circling with intent and may do what Cristiano Ronaldo had done with Manchester United a few years previously: promised one more campaign with the guarantee that he could secure his dream move the following season. The reality however was that the Uruguayan, from the moment he signed his new contract in December of 2013 (and firmly removed any lingering legal ambiguity) made the following few months merely an epilogue to his Liverpool career. The events at the World Cup when Suárez, after merrily destroying England, inexplicably bit Italy's Giorgio Chiellini, just made his departure all the more certain. The natural progression for elite footballing South Americans beckoned for the Uruguayan as he signed for Barcelona for £65 million in July. How, then, to replace such a player? In simple terms, this would be an impossibility but Liverpool looked to a player who appeared to possess some of Suarez's formidable gifts. Alexis Sánchez – a forward playing for the Catalans who would now surely struggle for game time – was seen as a natural replacement.

He was industrious, relentless, skilful, quick, the possessor of a devastating finish and Liverpool fans have since indulged in countless games of alternative history once Sánchez ended up signing for Arsenal. Some grumbled that Arsène Wenger had wooed the Chilean more effectively than a holidaying Rodgers, some still refuse to accept that Sánchez and his better half simply preferred the prospect of London's bright lights. Losing out on a transfer target was not a travesty – and was hardly unique to any club – but what still frustrates was the lack of a viable alternative. From all accounts, Liverpool ended up with a choice between Samuel Eto'o (now a Methuselah in modern, elite footballing terms) and Mario Balotelli. Surely there was someone out there, a player who possessed pace and imagination and could be acquired? A striker that could fit into the Liverpool ethos that Rodgers had built in the previous eighteen months?

But we still had one half of the feared SAS of the previous campaign and many wetted their lips in anticipation of Daniel Sturridge stepping up, of him relishing the prospect of being the star of the show.

Sturridge was injured with Hodgson's England in September and would effectively miss the majority of the campaign. After a steady if unspectacular opening to the new season, Liverpool now found themselves reliant on Balotelli, a forward of vast natural gifts but patently unsuited to the Reds' style or, indeed, playing up front on his own.

If the Reds' campaign of the previous year had been, to quote the reductionist mainstream media, a perfect storm, then this was starting to look like an equally flawless squall. But one with bleak, black clouds, pregnant with rain, seemingly perpetually on the horizon.

This is not hyperbole; those first few months of the 14/15 season felt that grim. The three Southampton players signed – Dejan Lovren, Rickie Lambert and Adam Lallana – all struggled, with the former rapidly gaining pariah status. Shorn of pace up front, with too much placed on the frail shoulders of Sterling, with Steven Gerrard finally looking like the ravages of time had caught up with him (and with a blueprint of how to negate his new position), with ceaseless, ineffective and sideways passing between Škrtel and Lovren, with Henderson struggling under his captain's gargantuan shadow and with Mignolet succumbing to a chronic bout of nerves, yes, it was depressing, dingy and grey. Balotelli was unable to score in the league, we all struggled with our confirmation bias and desperately looked for even an inkling that the Italian was adapting his game.

Lambert, after securing a dream move to his boyhood club, appeared to have aged roughly a decade during the summer. That winter, looking back, seems like a truly dark one and that there's almost certainly some trick being played on me by my brain, that it couldn't have been that bad. Well, the idea is not held up by even a cursory glance at the games.

Villa victorious at Anfield, a last gasp thunderbolt in the derby to deny us three much needed home points (and remember that free kick in the last minute to Everton?), a bonkers 3-2 victory over QPR when we made Bobby Zamora look like what we thought Mario actually was, the turgidity of the Hull scoreless draw in front of our frustrated fans, Newcastle United winning 1-0 in a game that was the definition of uninspired, Crystal Palace knocking three past us again but only conceding one this time. Then there was United in the middle of December and a display of festive charity from Brad Jones (in for the dropped Mignolet who now resembled a deer caught in the headlights of an onrushing galactic spaceship) who decided to dive the wrong way for Rooney's opener. And, let's face it, and not wishing to be overly harsh, was just as culpable for the other two in a 3-0 defeat. This result left the Reds in tenth position, eighteen points behind runaway leaders Chelsea and ten points adrift of

United who had, under the stewardship of Louis van Gaal, stuttered themselves.

Nor was there any solace to be had in the European arena. In the aftermath of the league title slipping away the previous summer, Liverpool fans had consoled themselves with the delicious prospect of a return to the Champions League after a five year hiatus. The group that the Reds were drawn in appeared to be infinitely traversable: fellow European aristocrats Real Madrid may have been daunting but Basel and Ludogorets Razgrad could surely not stop Liverpool from finishing in the top two? There is no need to discuss Liverpool's continental heritage here as we are all aware that swathes of the canvas that our history was painted upon were in Europe. But Rodgers – and, personally, this scribbler still thinks this is unfair and that there were extenuating circumstances – confirmed the view of many fans who were convinced that he would never succeed in European competition.

An unconvincing 2-1 victory (secured through a final minute penalty) against Ludogorets at Anfield was followed by a frankly depressing defeat to Basel in Switzerland. Already, hopes of qualification were starting to look tenuous, although Kopites could still hope that we may sneak second place. Despite being completely outclassed by Real Madrid and suffering a 3-0 defeat in late October, we were still offered some solace by Ludogorets beating Basel on the same night. Sandwiched between an Anfield defeat in the league by Chelsea – now looking like they were running away with the title – and that sobering, sterile performance at St James' Park when Newcastle deservedly won 1-0, the Reds had to travel to the Bernabéu to take on Madrid. Brendan Rodgers ensured Twitter virtually imploded in a mass of indignation as he picked a practical second string to take on the Spanish superclub. That they acquitted themselves well was forgotten; the narrative had been set and the die had been cast. A few months after nearly achieving immortality and delivering the Holy Grail, Rodgers looked like he was approaching burnout and was roundly castigated. It was hard, really, to see any of this ending favourably for the Northern Irishman.

However, despite elimination from the Champions League group stage being confirmed by a 2-2 home draw with Basel, Rodgers' and his side's fortunes were about to take an upswing. That 3-0 defeat to Manchester United may have been a nadir of the season thus far in terms of the final score, but the performance had been an encouraging one. The Liverpool manager deployed Sterling as a false nine with Coutinho just behind the flying youngster and, when Glen Johnson suffered an early injury, had replaced him with Kolo Touré. This was almost a 3-5-1-1 formation and set the template for an upsurge in form for Liverpool. Sterling had numerous chances in the Old Trafford fixture as did Balotelli when he came on; that David de Gea was man of the match spoke volumes. It looked like, finally, we may be onto something.

This feeling lasted beyond winter and well into spring as Liverpool suddenly became the form team in Europe. New Year's Day may have seen Leicester City, themselves firmly entrenched in a relegation battle, fight back from 2-0 down to secure an unlikely Anfield draw, but this result was overshadowed by the news that Gerrard would be leaving his beloved Reds at the end of the season. This announcement was met with more arguments from a fan base that was, yet again, labouring in division. Some were convinced that a still capable captain could deliver while some argued that he had succumbed to time and that his shadow was too vast – over the team and the manager. Regardless of the veracity of each argument, Gerrard was soon injured and would face a spell on the sidelines – a spell that coincided with a dramatic improvement in results.

Three more youngsters that had been signed the previous summer, Alberto Moreno, Lazar Marković and Emre Can, would be integral to this new formation which, for a while, bamboozled many a Premier League manager. The Spanish full-back had never really convinced as an unorthodox defender, but as a left wing back, with Markovic on the other flank, the team finally seemed to have some cohesion and identity. Emre Can also got an extended run in the side, playing in a back three but capable of becoming almost an auxiliary midfielder at times; his runs with the ball, vision and range of passing bode well for the future.

Despite a slightly unlucky exit in the League Cup Semi-Final at the hands of Chelsea, Liverpool continued to make progress in both the league and the FA Cup (when Slaven Bilić's Beşiktaş knocked the Reds out of the Europa League, not many were too upset). At the end of January, Daniel Sturridge returned to score the clinching second in a 2-0 victory over West Ham. There were now three games that appeared season defining on the horizon: lose any of these and the fight for fourth – which suddenly looked back on – would be dealt a fatal blow.

Tottenham were beaten 3-2 thanks to a late Balotelli winner. With Gerrard back in the side (although another slight injury was beckoning) and with Sturridge looking like he could finally turn the afterburners on again, it was a victory that gave huge cause for positivity. High flying Southampton were then, rather fortuitously, beaten 2-0 at St Mary's Park, an early Coutinho howitzer showing the Brazilian's maturity and capability from long range (though he could still frustrate).

In early March, another two bullets from Henderson and the Reds' mercurial Brazilian number ten secured a stirring 2-1 win over Manchester City. Suddenly, qualification for the Champions League and redemption for Rodgers and his team looked a real possibility although, somewhat prematurely, *The Independent* claimed that: '(the result) makes it likelier than not they will finish in the Champions League places.'

But it was one of those performances that Liverpool specialise in and one that had the whole of Anfield reverberating again. The result also all but confirmed Chelsea as Premier League champions and had both Manchester clubs gazing behind them with unease at an upwardly mobile Liverpool. When the Reds routinely dismantled Burnley a few days later they found themselves fifth in the table, two points behind Manchester United. Moreover, van Gaal's floundering side had to come to Anfield in a few weeks.

For many, Liverpool - not their northern rivals - were now favourites to secure at least fourth.

CHAPTER 22 - RUNNING OUT OF STEAM

Steven Gerrard was, in his own words, feeling 'like a caged animal' as, from the substitutes' bench, he gazed out despondently at what was transpiring on the Anfield pitch on a sun-dappled Sunday afternoon. Manchester United – now infinitely catchable by the Reds for the coveted fourth spot in the Premier League – were playing Liverpool off the park, their passing smooth, their pressing effective and relentless. Juan Mata had given the Reds' great rivals a fourteenth minute lead and Louis van Gaal looked to have completely countered Brendan Rodgers' system; a formation which may have yielded some months of fine form but had been partly exposed by the tactics of Swansea City a few days earlier. Now, the three at the back formation looked brittle and toothless as United relentlessly probed, cajoled and harassed.

One can imagine the seething frame of mind of the Liverpool captain as he witnessed what looked like something akin to tame capitulation against a club that – save from Everton – gave him the most abuse in the league; a side against whom he had both endured misery and excelled in triumph. Gerrard had been subjected to the familiar refrain of slipping and of not winning the league by a gleeful travelling support. Moreover, his role in the Liverpool side had been consistently questioned – both by a vocal media and his own support – and his much publicised departure from his beloved Reds was imminent. Perhaps there is little wonder that a red mist was hovering.

The match itself was to prove a turning point; the optimism of recent months of recovery was smothered as Gerrard launched himself into a scything tackle borne from bubbling frustration and was given his marching orders mere seconds after entering the fray. As he dejectedly made the long walk with his game over, so too, effectively, were Liverpool's hopes of catching their rivals and qualifying for the Champions League. United went 2-0 ahead, and though Daniel Sturridge pulled one back, it was always a mountain too steep to climb for the ten men. This may have been only one match but the Reds were now five points behind United and still had to face Arsenal at the Emirates the following week, where only a victory for Rodgers' beleaguered troops would salvage any lingering hopes of the coveted top four finish.

Instead, Liverpool were dismantled 4-1 by the Gunners in a display that symbolised everything that had gone wrong since the heady days of the previous season: hesitant shooting, bad decision making, lack of thrust (or, indeed, apparent trust in each other and quite possibly their manager), heads going down at the first sign of a setback. It was a tame surrender and signalled another miserable run of games as Liverpool ended the league campaign with eight points from their final nine matches. Two of these games in particular gained an instant grim notoriety and still inspire shivers of horror from Kopites everywhere. The unqualified horror show on the final day of the season as Liverpool were absolutely annihilated by Stoke City who ran out 6-1 winners (Liverpool's biggest league defeat since 1963) seemed to really break something within Brendan Rodgers. As he faced the media following this penny dreadful display, the Ulsterman looked haggard, haunted and stoically said that: 'if the owners want me to go, I go.'

The Stoke chastening had been Gerrard's last away game in the red shirt of Liverpool but his last home match didn't exactly see a legend given the send-off his contribution deserved. Anfield was awash with sentiment and nostalgia and there was discernible pride in the air but, alas, this never transmitted to the team as they abjectly surrendered 3-1 to a poor Crystal Palace side (aggregate score against the Londoners in the 14/15 season? 6-2.). There was no passion on display, no tenacity, and the disconnect that was present between the Liverpool side and its support was apparent when the Kop – with gallows scouse humour – greeted the captain's post-match assertion that the club would flourish in his absence with ironic laughter.

It had been hoped that Stevie's last appearance for the club he had served with such distinction would be an FA Cup Final on his birthday, a beguiling idea, dripping with romance as memories of forty yard screamers against West Ham resurfaced. Though the Reds had made progress in the competition it had been plodding rather than spectacular; replays against lower league opposition seemed to be a constant mid-week distraction during the spring. But Liverpool were given a glorious chance of making their captain's final appearance a showpiece Wembley one when they faced Aston Villa in the semi-final. The tie took place before the league abominations mentioned above and it was, for many, the point that Rodgers lost their faith. Despite the Reds taking a thirtieth minute lead through Coutinho, the Villains equalised soon after when Christian Benteke punished some typically shoddy defending. Early in the second half, Fabian Delph put Liverpool behind and Rodgers then tried what felt like roughly sixteen different formations and tactics in a vain attempt to force an equaliser. It may have been different if Balotelli hadn't been marginally ruled offside in the dying minutes, but the overriding memory of the cheerless resignation we all felt was Dejan Lovren's forty yard punt in injury time which nearly hit the Wembley roof.

As the season limped to its disheartening denouement, Rodgers had largely lost the fan base but as we entered the summer months, the silence from FSG was deafening – and more than a little telling. The axe was not ready to fall yet but two of the manager's backroom staff paid the price for the hugely disappointing campaign as Colin Pascoe and Mike Marsh were shown the door. In came Sean O'Driscoll and, perhaps in an attempt to appease some Kopites that were bordering on simmering rage, cult hero Gary McAllister. Some viewed this as a cowardly act by the Ulsterman, swerving a bullet by throwing colleagues under a bus, but in reality, what was he going to do? Despite the shock of Palace, Stoke and Villa, of a mauling by Arsenal and of finishing twenty five points behind Chelsea in sixth place, of shuffling and shambling towards the finish line as a miasma of dissatisfaction and disenchantment settled over the club, Rodgers believed in his abilities to turn the fortunes of his side around. In truth, he had earned another chance and, if he was no longer in credit, he was – as he claimed – around par.

But the Ulsterman's handling of situations was beginning to grate; many thought him arrogant, that he had been made to look better than he was by a footballing genius in 13/14 and had ridden this wave for all it was worth since. This may be entering into facile territory as there were many mitigating circumstances but Rodgers had made mistakes and it's probably fair to say that the arrows and slings of 14/15 had resulted in his sense of identity as a coach becoming compromised. The Liverpool manager had, quite possibly, looked at his reflection and blinked at what he saw staring back at him with haunted eyes.

It would be wrong to suggest that there was open revolt among the Liverpool supporters at FSG's decision to stick with their man but the summer of 2015 was one of those that have been all too frequent in recent years; fractures and division was the norm, wildly differing opinions existed on the terraces, in-fighting again became the status quo. There may have been a small minority that were prepared to give Brendan Rodgers a chance but his biggest issue was that as soon as he lost his first game, the knives would be out in force. Throughout those months, Liverpool supporters had to put up with the arcane opacity on the subject of transfers and this was another stick used to beat Rodgers with (retrospectively, probably fair enough given what has come to the surface since). The perceived wisdom is that the Liverpool manager wanted Christian Benteke, the towering Aston Villa striker, but that the committee was desperate to land the Brazilian attacker, Roberto Firmino. In the end, the club bought both and also brought in Nathaniel Clyne, Joe Gomez and Danny Ings while James Milner, the industrious and talented Man City midfielder arrived on a free transfer (but earning a considerable wage). FSG, it would appear, were clearly backing their manager in the market.

The one significant departure from the playing staff saw Raheem Sterling – after a protracted and increasingly acrimonious stand-off between he and the club over a new contract – leave for Manchester City for just under £50 million. From the point of view of both Sterling and Liverpool Football Club, there were mistakes made in the episode developing into a saga but the shenanigans of Sterling's agent, Adie Ward, left a bitter taste.

As often happens in football, the fixture computer threw up an intriguing test for Rodgers and his side in the first game of the 15/16 campaign as the Reds travelled back to Stoke – scene of that sobering trouncing and possibly the manager's worst afternoon in football. The game – a fairly sterile affair – was decided by a piece of Coutinho magic as he rolled his marker and hammered home a twenty five yard strike into the top corner with minutes remaining. Next up, newly promoted Bournemouth were slightly unfortunate to find themselves beaten by Benteke's first Liverpool goal but it was the first half performance against Arsenal in the Emirates that had many wondering if Rodgers had rediscovered his Midas touch. The Reds' mercurial number ten – now clearly improving in front of our eyes and becoming a genuine match winner – was desperately unlucky not to score and Benteke somehow saw his shot from a yard or two out saved by Cech. In the second half Liverpool dug deep and a disciplined performance meant a share of the points. The team looked to be playing with a degree of confidence and, if not seamless going forward, appeared to have gelled in defence. The youngster Gomez was assured at left-back, Clyne was consistency made manifest on the other flank while even the much maligned Lovren looked to have put his struggles behind him. Seven points from the opening three games was an excellent return and there was some guarded optimism around Anfield as the first international break ended proceedings for a fortnight.

When the Premier League returned, the Reds returned to earth with a shuddering bang. West Ham arrived in Liverpool and were promptly 2-0 ahead within thirty minutes; the second goal showing Lovren at his absolute hesitant worst. The demons of the previous season – far from being exorcised – were now abounding as the terraces shook with trepidation and angst. Coutinho was soon sent off and a third goal was conceded against Bilić's new side. All the old problems were evidently to the fore and the writing was beginning to look like it was on the wall for Rodgers already. A chance at some sort of redemption was spectacularly not taken as the Reds travelled to Old Trafford next and were dismissed by a dull United in possibly one of the most turgid encounters between the two great rivals in recent years. Rodgers appeared the very apotheosis of a manager living on borrowed time, unsure of himself and his methods as Danny Ings was deployed as a practical left-back. As *The Times* put it:

There are times in a manager's career when the victories barely register and when every loss leaves another scar. This campaign always threatened to be like that for Brendan Rodgers. The Liverpool manager claimed that a line had been drawn under last season's tribulations, but this limp defeat, at Old Trafford of all places, only added to an alarming sense of drift.'

There was no respite to be had for the Ulsterman; three draws in three different competitions followed (lowly Carlisle United needed a penalty shoot out to be knocked out of the League Cup) before Sturridge's latest injury comeback lit up a 3-2 victory against Aston Villa, comfortably the worst team in the division at this stage. A further two 1-1 draws in the space of three days in early October, against Sion in the Europa League and Everton at Goodison Park in the Premier League, meant that the team and its support were firmly entrenched in a mire of mediocrity. But Rodgers may well have gotten a stay of execution if not for the availability of a certain German. This is a story that began a few months prior and would develop into a narrative of thrilling proportions for all Kopites.

CHAPTER 23 - FROM DOUBTERS TO BELIEVERS

In October of 2014 – just as Brendan Rodgers' Liverpool were beginning to wake up to the sobering reality that was post-Suárez and post-title charge – Borussia Dortmund, under the stewardship of Jürgen Klopp, were enduring their worst run of form since the enigmatic and charismatic manager had taken the helm. Five consecutive defeats saw the club plummet to seventeenth in the Bundesliga. As Elmar Nevelling wrote in his biography of Klopp, with prophetic echoes that would follow the German to England in the fullness of time:

Time and again, Dortmund were finding themselves struggling to break down teams who were (successfully) attempting to stifle their tactics through parking the metaphorical bus in front of goal. Bayern and Borussia Mönchengladbach were almost the only teams not to attempt this, being confident that they could beat Dortmund their own way.'

Following years of rampant success, Klopp's Dortmund were on a downward trajectory. Perhaps it was that Klopp's shelf life as a manager of the side had been reached and breached, perhaps a counter to his tactics had been discovered by his rivals, perhaps losing the likes of Robert Lewandowski and Mario Götze to Bayern had been too difficult to recover from. Klopp himself blamed the severe injuries that struck his team that autumn; by November Nuri Sahin, Ilkay Gündogan, Jacub Blaszczykowski, Oliver Kirch and Marco Reus were all out for substantial periods. Though Dortmund would recover following the *Hinrunde* and winter break, by early April the former Bundesliga champions were languishing in tenth place.

On the 15th April, four days before one of the low points of Rodgers' Liverpool career would unfold with that FA Cup Semi-Final defeat to Aston Villa, Borussia announced that there would be a press conference. Ever since *die Schwarzgelben* had hovered above the relegation zone, Dortmund's CEO (and Klopp's close personal friend), Hans-Joachim Watzke, had feared that the manager 'well known for being emotional, would resign.' These fears were about to be realised as a clearly affected

Watzke faced the media and imparted the news that put most of the heavy hitting clubs in Europe on red alert:

'…following Jürgen Klopp's initiative, we have conducted several intense conversations over the last few days and then reached the mutual decision that the path we have been travelling on for seven long years with unbelievable success will come to a conclusion at the end of the season.'

Dortmund's Director of Football, Michael Zorc, was also present and waxed lyrical on the impact Klopp had had on the club as he claimed that 'Over the last seven years we have written a modern football fairy tale, with Jürgen Klopp playing the main role. In 2008, we weren't in good sporting condition, but you gave this club huge optimism.'

For his part, the departing manager stated, with typical honesty and earnestness, that he was: 'no longer the perfect manager for this extraordinary club, which deserves to be managed by the coach who is 100 percent perfect for it.'

Following the announcement, Dortmund remained unbeaten for the rest of the season and reached the German Cup Final, beating their biggest rivals Bayern Munich on penalties in the semis (*die Schwarzgelben* would lose in the final itself to Wolfsburg, continuing Klopp's less than stellar record in finals).

Klopp seemed at peace, and with grimly ironic humour that would soon become very familiar to football fans in England, announced that 'if I'd known before the start of the season that we'd put such a run together, I'd have announced my departure back then. Seventh place feels brilliant.'

There may have been more than a degree of sarcasm in the German's claims but Dortmund's final league position ensured Europa League football for his successor the following season; a scenario that would eventually bring a thrilling sense of serendipity to Liverpool fans.

For the next few months, as speculation intensified over the then Liverpool manager's position, Jürgen Klopp and his assistants Zeljko Buvac and Peter Krawietz took a well-earned sabbatical – their first break in fourteen years. As Klopp's agent, Marc Kosicke, said at the time:

Jürgen has two great loves in his past, and it's difficult to jump right into the next relationship. He wants to feel like a "single manager" and experience things with his wife that he hasn't had time for in a while. That need became increasingly strong.'

There was, predictably enough, widespread speculation linking Klopp with every big club over the next few months and Liverpool was seen as a potential destination throughout the summer of 2015. Could the Anfield club, if they decided to dispense with the services of Brendan Rodgers, attract such a stellar name, a genuine world class coach, when the titans of the European game were all mooted as potential employers? The likely reality, of course, is that Klopp never really wanted a job like Real, City or Chelsea. A deeply anti-establishment figure, he didn't see himself coming in, the latest big name, world-renowned coach, and routinely winning a league before getting sacked. The only possible exception to this was perhaps Bayern because he was (and is) adored in Germany, by far the most popular and charismatic manager in the country, the cult of the personality incarnate and a figure whose face could be seen on billboards and on TV advertisements throughout Germany.

Undoubtedly, Klopp also saw massive parallels between Liverpool and Dortmund: colossal history but not the richest, messianic almost religious fervour of fans, working class and socialist city, huge challenge to restore past glories. It would be fair to surmise that Klopp had no interest in carrying on from a Pellegrini or Mourinho or Luis Enrique to gather expected trophies. He had talked before about creating a legacy, his own dynasty in the face of huge odds. That, in many ways, was and is his modus operandi. When the Reds played Dortmund in a friendly during the summer of 2014, the German had stood, transfixed, listening to the Kop sing. He then asked for a private tour and spent two hours in the trophy room. Klopp wanted a project, to overcome the odds, to bring down the super powers, to entertain and to be loved. In many ways, Liverpool was the perfect fit for Jürgen Klopp.

As mentioned previously, the 1-1 derby draw in Goodison Park would prove to be Brendan Rodgers' last game in charge of the Reds. At the time, Liverpool were tenth in the Premier League, having taken twelve points from their opening eight games. None of us know what went on behind the scenes, despite constant speculation since, but what is beyond doubt is that FSG moved quickly to secure their man. Given the depth of backing Rodgers had received from the Liverpool ownership the previous summer, the unfolding events of that Sunday, October 4th, were surprising but John Henry probably knew that this was a one off chance to get a bona fide world class manager. That afternoon the official website said that the Ulsterman 'will leave his post with immediate effect after having his contract terminated' and that the process of finding a successor was 'underway' and that 'we hope to make an appointment in a decisive and timely manner.' The club went on to say of the departing manager:

We would like to place on record our sincere thanks to Brendan Rodgers for the significant contribution he has made to the club and express our gratitude for his hard work and commitment. All of us have experienced some wonderful moments with Brendan as manager, and we are confident he will enjoy a long career in the game. Although this has been a difficult decision, we believe it provides us with the best opportunity for success on the pitch. Ambition and winning are at the heart of what we want to bring to Liverpool and we believe this change gives us the best opportunity to deliver it.'

There has been a great deal of revisionism since Rodgers left Liverpool but the reality is that, for at least half of his time at the helm, he did a fine job and produced winning, attractive football from his side. He was a relatively inexperienced manager when he took the job and his assertion about putting together an aeroplane while trying to fly it was probably a good analogy of the unique difficulty presented by the job of Liverpool manager – perhaps the most challenging role in modern football. But he proved himself to be adaptable, to be flexible in his tactics. That some fans never took to him cannot be denied nor can the fact that his personal life and desire to improve his appearance inexplicably had the moralists out in force. But he should never be forgotten for 13/14; a season when Brendan Rodgers came agonisingly close to footballing immortality. Yes, Suárez played a huge part in the success of that campaign but it was Rodgers who unleashed the system which got the best from the Uruguayan's exceptional and peerless talents. Sterling blossomed under the Ulsterman's stewardship, Coutinho started his march towards world class and Daniel Sturridge, hitherto unconvincing at Manchester City and Chelsea, became the best English striker around. (That the latter two were secured by the transfer committee is almost certain. But that shouldn't ignore the fact that Rodgers got a huge amount from their distinctive gifts).

By the time Liverpool lost Suárez to Barcelona and Sturridge to injury in 2014/15, it is very possible that Rodgers had been scarred by the capitulation to Crystal Palace at the end of the previous campaign; certainly, something seemed to change in the Ulsterman's demeanour and tactics. Perhaps the ultimate tragedy of his time in charge was that he just didn't possess the conviction to stick with his original philosophy – he looked in the mirror, and saw the gorgon.

Fans and media alike were giddy with conjecture as the ITKs on social media went into overdrive but by the Tuesday it was all but certain that Jürgen Klopp would be the new Liverpool manager. He was officially unveiled on Friday, the 8th October with a press conference that sizzled and popped with the German's charisma, humour and confidence. His talk of being 'the normal one' raised a laugh with everyone and, as we permitted ourselves to smile at his self-effacement, the feelings of division within the fan base appeared to evaporate. Finally Liverpool fans, who take the cult of the manager more seriously than any other, could be united under an inspirational banner, a coach who seemed tailor made for this unique city and football club. Here was a genuine world class manager, who wanted to be at our club, who got it. The anticipation was as thrilling as it was palpable.

Klopp would have to wait for his first game as Liverpool manager as another exercise in irrelevance that is the international break delayed the German's charges from taking to the field. Frustratingly, Danny Ings and Joe Gomez were struck down with season-ending injuries and Sturridge would also be ruled out for a period. Klopp's first game was a creditable 0-0 draw with Spurs but a glance at the substitutes' bench on that windy

October afternoon demonstrated the job that the German had inherited as Jerome Sinclair, Adam Bogdan, Kolo Touré, Connor Randall, João Carlos Teixeira, Jordan Ibe and Joe Allen all looked on from the sidelines; a few months later, none of these would be at the club. Three fairly uninspiring results in three different competitions then followed before a game that felt like Klopp had truly arrived as a stumbling Chelsea - defending Premier League champions - welcomed the Reds to Stamford Bridge. A Coutinho brace and a clincher from Benteke gave Liverpool a superb 3-1 victory (the rot had yet to fully set in with Mourinho's Blues at this stage and football fans didn't as yet know how bad it would get for the Londoners). Crystal Palace - bogey club supreme - then came to Anfield and gave Klopp a first hand account of the bruising and bustling idiosyncrasies of the English Premier League as they left Liverpool with a 2-1 victory. The rollercoaster of the Reds' first few months under the German continued with an emphatic and thrilling 4-1 win over Manchester City, with Lallana, Coutinho and Firmino dovetailing to devastating effect. When Southampton were then battered 6-1 at St Mary's in the League Cup Quarter-Final, embryonic talk of a late title surge began to take root by some. Typically though, Liverpool assisted even the most optimistic fans in staying firmly grounded as a dire Newcastle United side - heading inexorably towards relegation under Steve McClaren - defeated Liverpool 2-0 at St James's Park. As the festive period beckoned, Martin Škrtel then effectively signed his own death warrant in a red shirt with an abject, cowardly display, allowing himself to be bullied by the Watford forwards as the Hornets defeated Liverpool 3-0; possibly still the lowest point of Klopp's time with the Reds. The league campaign would stumble on for the rest of the season with some notable results followed by ineffectual displays. But by March, it had become clear that the Europa League - long derided by the majority of English supporters - was the best chance Liverpool had of qualifying for the Champions League the following season.

The Reds had successfully negotiated a relatively straightforward group and drew Augsburg in the first knock-out round. A 1-0 aggregate win was hardly inspiring but the competition - and Liverpool's European form - was about to significantly heat up. Manchester United, who were struggling in the league themselves in van Gaal's last season in charge, were then pitted against the Reds for a place in the quarter-finals. In a heaving Anfield in early March, the two great rivals met as the Europa League suddenly became a hugely desirable prize. Liverpool were superb and gained some revenge for their league defeat a few weeks previously as a Sturridge penalty and late Firmino goal gave the Reds a 2-0 victory. The return tie a week later was a different matter with United gaining a one goal lead and looking uncharacteristically threatening until an exquisite goal from Coutinho silenced Old Trafford and made the second half a formality. With curious, but somehow inevitable, happenstance Klopp's former side, Borussia Dortmund, were then drawn in the quarter-final. If the first leg in Germany, an encouraging 1-1 draw, was routine, the return game at Anfield was one of those special, special European nights - nights that Liverpool seem to specialise in. Epic, historic, shiver-inducing: perhaps these superlatives aren't used now because of how the Reds ultimately ended the competition. But make no mistake, this thrilling and memorable contest was what makes it so great to be a football fan. Despite how we're programmed to believe, sometimes the journey is better than the destination and though modern Liverpool may sometimes feel like a bewildering mosaic of falling at the final hurdle, sometimes that's ok. Sometimes a game like this is the reason we put up with every disappointment and every argument and every depressing arrow of misfortune.

Dortmund, a formidable outfit boasting talent that were being enviously eyed throughout the continent, gave Liverpool a lesson in attacking at speed and controlled aggression in the opening parts of the match. Mkhitaryan and Pierre-Emerick Aubameyang gave the Germans a 2-0 lead and meant the Reds now needed to score three times. Though Divock Origi - in the midst of his first real rich vein of form since his arrival - seemed to give Liverpool a fighting chance early in the second half, the brilliant Marco Reus then produced a sublime finish to surely take the tie out of Liverpool's hands. Even a marvellously adroit goal from Coutinho could only be a mere consolation? But when Sakho headed in from a corner with twelve minutes left, Liverpool fans at Anfield and throughout the world sensed we may be on the cusp - yet again - of something special. Dortmund players looked panicked, shell shocked, as they sought to stem the tide of noise and passion and destiny that was unfurling around them. The players in red responded to the gorgeous, deafening entreaties of a howling and bellowing crowd and in injury time, with the Germans perhaps feeling that they had gotten through the gauntlet of desire and magic that was Anfield that night, that they may have just escaped, Dejan Lovren rose to head James Milner's cross into the net. Pandemonium ensued in every bastion of red, in every home and pub and club where this beguiling contest was being shown. Anfield - scene of so many unforgettable nights - had just witnessed another.

Following these heroics, the semi-final against Villarreal was more prosaic; despite conceding a late goal in Spain to seemingly give the Spanish outfit the advantage, Liverpool were magnificent in Anfield again and ran out 3-0 winners. The Reds' reward for this thoroughly dominating performance was a place in the final with serial winners of the competition, Sevilla. Daniel Sturridge's exquisite, improbable and inexplicable goal deserves to be remembered more fondly but the bewildering second half capitulation by Liverpool meant that this moment of genius would be consigned to a footnote of our European history. This collapse and subsequent defeat would provide harsh lessons for Klopp, lessons that would be digested and acted upon.

The finale of Klopp's first partial campaign in charge may have been anticlimactic and heart-rending in the extreme, but Liverpool fans still looked forward to the new season with bated breath. That summer the footballing festivities of the European Championships in France took place with a not inconsiderable spectre of terrorism hanging over it as the world seemed to lurch from one calamity to the next. David Cameron's ultimately doomed game of Russian Roulette with a nation's future led millions waking up in June facing a most uncertain future as Brexit became a bemusing and dismaying reality. The trials and tribulations of a football club were put into perspective as events became ever more troubling throughout the planet but, almost paradoxically, the Reds were about to give some form of solace to many as they refused to let the claustrophobic and pungent cloud of alarm that felt like it was enveloping everywhere from affecting their brilliance. Liverpool were, in the opening few months of the new campaign, the perfect tonic to Trump's perplexing victory or to the general politics of fear and hatred that suddenly seemed all encompassing. Years before, as the Cold War had threatened to heat up, then FIFA president Stanley Rous had memorably claimed that 'in a world haunted by the hydrogen and napalm bomb, the football field is a place where sanity and hope are left unmolested.' In the theatre of modern football, this may have been stretching it, but, as the Reds lit up football pitches throughout the autumn and early winter, the sentiment was an apt one.

But for all that was to come, the transfer dealings conducted by the club left many Liverpool supporters distinctly underwhelmed. With the curious, antagonistic fervour that grips most football fans who have never essentially witnessed the skill of a player, it was those that didn't actually arrive that caused the most consternation. Klopp failed to get his reported biggest targets such as Mario Götze, Mahmoud Dahoud, Piotr Zielenski and Ousmane Dembélé but managed to acquire a triumvirate of players that would play a huge role in the upcoming campaign. Sadio Mané arrived from Southampton having recently taken Robbie Fowler's record for quickest Premier League hat-trick, Georginio Wijnaldum was bought from relegated Newcastle United and Jöel Matip came in on a free transfer from Schalke. Jürgen Klopp also raided his homeland (and former club) for Loris Karius who may have endured a mixed start but is a goalkeeper who it would appear has Klopp's full confidence and backing. Mamadou Sakho - one of the heroes of the Europa League run - had been (ultimately) falsely and opaquely accused of failing a drugs test the previous summer by UEFA. This saga would cost the French defender a place in both his country's

European Championship campaign and Liverpool's Europa League Final. However, rumblings of ill-discipline continued and following Sakho being sent home from a pre-season tour in America, it became apparent that he had no place in Klopp's plans; he would be banished to the reserves and eventually sent on loan to Crystal Palace. Also departing to Palace was Christian Benteke, who had never fully convinced under the German manager and his preferred system. Other notable departures were Joe Allen and a disappointing Jordan Ibe to Stoke City and Bournemouth respectively.

The Premier League big hitters, still reeling from Leicester City's improbable triumph a few months earlier, were about to reassert themselves and the formation of a genuine big six was to become a reality in 2016/17. It would take a gargantuan effort just to finish in the top four; two very good sides that would previously have deserved to take their place in the Champions League were now sure to miss out. But as the bright autumn months unfolded before us, Liverpool fans started to dream big again. Could the title be a reality? A thrilling win against one of our biggest rivals on the opening day of the season set the scene; Arsène Wenger looked on with a haggard and terrified face as Sadio Mané announced himself to his new adoring public as he took on what seemed like the entire Arsenal defence and fired past Cech to make it 4-1. Pace, verve, skill and emphatic finishing were all to the fore as the Senegalese forward bullied and terrified the Gunners' rearguard. The game finished 4-3 and was, in hindsight, the season in microcosm as Liverpool thrilled going forward but were less convincing at the back; a malady now afflicting the Reds since Kenny's only full campaign in charge. A credible draw away to Spurs in which three points were perhaps deserved by Klopp's side was followed by a total dismantling of the Premier League champions as Leicester were summarily dismissed at Anfield's first game of the season. Glorious images of the new stand bedecked in red in the bright sun still play in the mind as Firmino, Mané and Lallana ruthlessly slaughtered the Foxes. Liverpool were simply irrepressible for the next few months; a bewildering, dancing and joyous crescendo of attacking brilliance as teams were routinely put to the sword. The front three of Mané, Coutinho and Firmino was one of the most fluid and interchangeable attacks in Europe and fear and trepidation was tangible in the opposition as the thrilling troika took to the field. With the captain Jordan Henderson operating as the deepest midfielder and setting the pace and Adam Lallana also dropping deeper to brilliant effect, Anfield was awash with optimism and talk of a genuine crack at that agonisingly elusive Premier League title. The Reds topped the table in early November as Watford were obliterated 6-1; a scoreline that actually flattered the Hornets. Daniel Sturridge, fit now but unable to get a starting berth in Klopp's side, came on and was effervescent and perhaps unlucky not to score a hat-trick.

Kopites drooled over this apparent new found strength in depth as the England striker, along with Emre Can and Divock Origi, were fixtures on the bench in those early months; the beguiling staccato of Klopp's system not compatible – at least in the early months – with their talents.

But even at the height of Liverpool fans' buoyancy over a potential title, there was no escaping the fact that the competition would be fierce – perhaps the most competitive since the inception of the Premier League. As the TV money being pumped into the English game now started to move beyond fantastical and enter the realms of the obscene, the managerial landscape was now a fearsome one.

Joining Klopp, Wenger and Tottenham's startlingly impressive Mauricio Pochettino were Pep Guardiola, principle shaper of possibly the most impressive club side of all time, the serial winning Italian Antonio Conte and old foe Mourinho. Pep's Manchester City started with a bang as they recorded win after win in the autumn months and though Conte appeared to slightly struggle early in his Chelsea career, he soon brought in his favoured 3-5-1-1 system with spectacular and historic results; a formation change that proved so effective that most other sides in the league flirted with it. Mourinho's early months (and, indeed, the majority of his domestic campaign) may have been underwhelming but the wily and abrasive Portuguese had broken the world transfer record to bring back United graduate Paul Pogba from Juventus. For good measure, the Manchester club also added former Liverpool target and current German Player of the Year, Henrikh Mkhitaryan, to their ranks while also recruiting a little known Swede by the name of Zlatan Ibrahimovic.

Talk of a genuine shot at winning the Premier League had barely coalesced outside Anfield when the whisperings were kept quiet as the Reds suffered their second defeat of the season to Bournemouth in December. This 4-3 defeat could perhaps be written off as one of those mad, topsy turvy games that happen in a season but there was now an emerging, disquieting feeling that the flexibility and fluid attacking, of the relentless and dogged pressing that had characterised the early part of the season, was losing some of its lustre. Had Klopp's tactics been, to a degree, figured out and had opposition teams learned how to nullify the threat posed by the Reds? Many asked themselves this question but, nevertheless, the Christmas period was a fine one for Liverpool as they took ten points from a possible twelve, including a late, shiver-inducing winner by Mané in the Goodison derby and a spirited and intransigent 1-0 victory over Manchester City at Anfield on New Year's Eve. However, with Chelsea continuing to churn out victory after victory, a 2-2 draw against perennial recent strugglers Sunderland turned disquiet into a species of foreboding. If we were to realistically catch the London club, there was no margin for error. The new world of social media gave voice to the venting of fans that had perhaps gotten carried away with the fine start to the campaign; nothing less than a resounding win would now prevent a Twitter meltdown.

But Twitter hadn't really seen anything yet; January was a diabolically bad month, even for those Liverpool fans grounded in pragmatism. A run of ten games without a victory saw the Reds topple out of two competitions and costly defeats in the league to Swansea and Hull (in early February) rang the death knell for any lingering hopes of reeling in Chelsea. The impact of Coutinho's and Lallana's injuries, suffered before Christmas, were depressingly consolidated by the absence of Mané to the African Cup of Nations; the prior notion that the Reds had strength in depth proving to have no more substance than gossamer wings. But Liverpool rallied and beat Spurs convincingly at Anfield as Sadio Mané ran amok and it looked like the Reds may be getting back to the fizz and sparkle of the first half of the season. Alas, Leicester City then bludgeoned their way to a 3-1 win as Klopp's charges seemed to succumb to peripheral intimidation tactics. Hard fought wins over Arsenal and Burnley at Anfield restored a degree of confidence in the Reds' ability to finish in the all-important top four places and this sense of progress was consolidated in a frenetic 1-1 draw with Manchester City at the Etihad; a game just as noticeable for the glaring misses from both sides as it was for the almost impossibly high intensity of the match. Following another tortuous international break, the Reds resumed their drive for Champions League places with a resounding 3-1 win over Everton as Coutinho and Mané thrilled the home fans; alas, it was to prove to be the latter's last contribution to a hugely impressive debut season as injury struck arguably Liverpool's best player.

The final strait now beckoned for Jürgen Klopp and his team as they faced a run in of eight games that looked, on paper at least, infinitely winnable. However, modern Liverpool doesn't do things the easy way and almost seem to insist on making it hard for themselves. Having convincingly topped the mini-league of head-to-heads with the top six, the Reds travails against the bottom ten clubs was well documented. This view was given added credence as Liverpool laboured to a 2-2 draw at home to Bournemouth and seemed to be handing the initiative to Arsenal, United and City in the race for the final two spots to qualify for Europe's premier competition. But Liverpool's rivals were just as inconsistent and just as capable of dropping their own momentum and two back-to-back away victories – the very definition of hard fought – over Stoke and West Bromwich Albion put the Reds' Champions League fate back in their own hands. However, the disjointed nature of the last weeks of the campaign was writ large as Crystal Palace defeated an insipid and toothless Liverpool at Anfield. Did anyone actually want to finish in the top four?

Another tricky away day now loomed as Watford – a team of giants – waited just north of London. Though the Reds were far from their buccaneering best, a goal of pure genius from Emre Can (and eventual goal of the season winner), now playing some of the best football of his Anfield career, settled the contest but more frustration followed as James Milner uncharacteristically missing a penalty meant Southampton held Liverpool to a 0-0 draw. Briefly, Liverpool's fate was out of their own hands but Arsenal, in the midst of a typical late season surge, then beat a dull and distracted United. The remit for Liverpool was now simple: win the two remaining league game to guarantee the return of Champions League football.

Foreboding was tangible amongst Liverpool fans as the season entered its last week; surely, after practically spending the entire season in the top four, they couldn't throw it away now? Kopites looked on with irritation as Arsenal convincingly swept aside a flip-flop wearing Stoke City at the Britannia Stadium the day before the Reds travelled to London to take on an injury-ravaged West Ham. There was now no margin for error but, shorn of Roberto Firmino, Klopp played a diamond with Sturridge and Origi up front and Coutinho operating deeper than usual. It proved a masterstroke as Liverpool ran out 4-0 winners; perhaps they received some good fortune from the officials and a somewhat less than fully competitive opposition, but this had been earned throughout the rest of the campaign. The final game of the season was one that was almost anomalous in the Premier League era; a game for the Reds with something at stake. And what a prize to fight for: a spot at Europe's top table and the chance to prevent Arsenal from dining at it for the first time in twenty years. To those weaned on the halcyon days of success after success, this scenario may have been underwhelming but the reality was that, for Klopp to continue his progress and for the project to keep driving forward, qualification for the Champions League was a must. Liverpool didn't disappoint and despite a nervy first half, eventually asserted their authority and superior ability with goals from Wijnaldum, Coutinho and Lallana giving the home side a 3-0 victory.

The season's goals had been met but the work had only just begun.

EPILOGUE: HOW GOLDEN IS THAT SKY?

An unheralded Norwich City midfielder by the name of Jeremy Goss may be an odd place to start any conclusion of Liverpool's journey in English football's modern era, but in many ways the Welsh 'Gossa' perfectly illustrates the tectonic shift between the birth of the Premier League and the strange country we all find ourselves inhabiting now. Moreover, of course, it was the Welshman's goal that was to prove to be the last one ever scored at the old Spion Kop in 1994.

A few months previously, Goss's Canaries - who finished third in the inaugural Premier League campaign behind Manchester United and Aston Villa - travelled to Bayern Munich's Olympiastadion and inflicted the Bavarian club's only ever defeat by a British side on German soil. Goss scored a thundering opener, lashing home a volley in that UEFA Cup Second Round tie to help secure an historic 2-1 victory. Improbably to our eyes - weaned, as we have been, on a cavalcade of foreign talent - that Norwich City team contained just one non-British player: Ruel Fox, who had been born on the Caribbean island of Montserrat. Clearly the claws of money being relentlessly pumped into Sky Sports' flagship had yet to truly sink in but the English game was undergoing a violent metamorphosis. It would emerge from this shifting cocoon as more entertaining, as a thrilling, pulse-quickening creature and with stadiums that are infinitely safer and more welcoming. But domestic football did not emerge unscathed and a Mephistophelean deal was a by-product of the entire process. For Liverpool Football Club, conservative and family run, loathe to embrace modern values and, in some ways, whose owners fought against this evolutionary voyage, the birth pangs of the Premier League were troubling and turbulent indeed.

On 30th April, 1994, mere weeks before Diana Ross would fail to find the net in a garish opening ceremony to the World Cup in the US - a ceremony that seemed to predict the direction football was travelling in - Goss scored the winner for Norwich City as the Reds fell to a 1-0 defeat in their last home game of the season. Anfield was about to be forever changed as, following the Taylor report, the first shoots of true modernity began to make their way through the football club: the stadium was to become an all-seater and the old standing Kop was about to be demolished.

It's easy to take for granted just how much the world - not just football - has changed since that day. That was the year that Kurt Cobain died and *Four Weddings and a Funeral* took the planet by storm, that Oasis' *Definitely Maybe* and Blur's *Parklife* helped start the Britpop phenomenon. Sony launched the original, seemingly miraculous PlayStation and Tarantino truly became the next hip director with *Pulp Fiction*. In 1994, there were around sixty seven mobile phones for every one thousand people in Britain. OJ Simpson was chased through Los Angeles live on TV, a strange precursor to a World Cup where Diego Maradona was sent home in disgrace, a newly unified Germany was beaten by a Yordan Letchkov header and the Colombian Andres Escobar was shot dead. The prospect of a World Wide Web started to really gather momentum as the relatively short lived Netscape Navigator was released. Also apparently gathering momentum were relations with Britain and the continent, as the Channel Tunnel was officially opened. By 2016, of course - and due to a plethora of complex factors - Brexit was a troubling reality as the British mindset appeared to come full circle.

But on that day in late spring, as Liverpool - holder of a record number of league titles and who had been champions just four years previously - were about to finish eighth in the second ever Premier League, only one thing mattered to a heaving Anfield. Writing in LFCHistory.net, author Sigfús Guttormsson took up the tale:

'A big festival took place before, during and after the game between Liverpool and Norwich City. The Kop was simply magnificent this sunny spring day. 44,339 filled Anfield on the day and there were probably about 16,000 on The Kop itself. The Canaries' boss John Deehan received an unusual request from the Reds before the game. He was asked to let the Reds attack the Kop in the second half. John had no problem with that! The players couldn't quite match the brilliance of the crowd and Liverpool lost 1-0. The Welshman, Jeremy Goss, scored the only goal and became the last player to score in front of The Kop.

The famous old terrace was a sight to behold. The flags, the banners, the colour and the singing. This was a highly emotional afternoon and there was more than a tear or two in the eyes of some old and young Kopites. The standing Kop was the man of the match! Not for the first time but the last!

The day after a big concert was held on The Kop. Many of Liverpool's most famous bands performed. At the end of the concert the standing Kop sang "You'll Never Walk Alone" for the last time. A few days later work started on taking the most famous terrace in the world down. A new stand, which holds 12,390 spectators, was built during the summer of 1994.'

Just over twenty years later - in December 2014 - work finally began on the club's new main stand. Liverpool chairman, Tom Werner, was ebullient on the subject:

'It was just over two years ago that we said our preference was to stay at Anfield and here we are announcing that the expansion is going ahead. We have made more progress in the past two years than in the past decade. Having experience of expanding Fenway Park, and having been through a similar and very successful project with the Red Sox, everyone at FSG is extremely proud and excited to be part of expanding Anfield stadium.'

The road to this development had been, to say the very least and to put it mildly, a chequered one and bookended highs and lows on the pitch. Originally mooted in May of 2002, just as Houllier's Reds were finishing a hugely encouraging second in the Premier League, it was envisaged that a 55,000 capacity stadium would be constructed in Stanley Park. At the time the club felt it was prohibitively difficult to improve Anfield and so plans were made to build a bowl shaped arena a mere three hundred yards away from the original ground. Rick Parry had claimed that the logistics of developing on Anfield itself - and he mentioned the Main Stand specifically - would be too difficult to complete. Amid whisperings of ground sharing with Everton, this was eventually abandoned and it then became clear that new ownership of the club was being sought. George Gillett briefly breathed life into the Stanley Park project when, a couple of months before a Champions League Final in Athens, he infamously and desultorily promised that 'the spade has to be in the ground.' By May of the following year this claim was proven to be as insubstantial as the Hicks and Gillett regime as construction was halted. It would take what the Texans oxymoronically called 'an epic swindle,' with New England Sports Ventures taking control of the club, for the wheels to be again set in motion for the development of Anfield.

On a beautifully golden autumn's evening on the 10th of September 2016, Anfield was a glorious, bouncing and gorgeous sight as the new £115 million Main Stand was unveiled. A crowd of 53,074 - the biggest in thirty nine years, when the Reds won the 1977 League Championship - looked on as Liverpool destroyed Leicester City, to give some indication of the football that would be served up in those early months of the campaign. The new look stadium, imposing, towering and pristine all at once, seemed to give Anfield new buoyancy and a fresh sense of optimism. The football may have been majestic at times, but it was the regality of the almost totemic Main Stand that also helped to suffuse the fans with delicious anticipation and pride. Suddenly, Liverpool had an imposing structure, worthy of their stature and it was a tangible sign of progress. Klopp had acknowledged the potential for harnessing the extra fans in the stadium before the match when he said that 'eight thousand more in the stadium...or something like this, yeah, that's more power.' He was equally as effusive in his post-match interview when he noted that Anfield was 'so different, so nice, so big, it's everything and we all love nice and wonderful stadiums so that was really good. So we knew that we had to do a job today, and that's what we did against a strong opponent.' In what was by now a familiar theme for the German, he also stressed the importance of utilising the unique ardour and zeal that the Anfield crowd could project; this doubly so, now that there was far more potential for clamour and dissonance: 'We need to have atmospheres like this, not only against the champions when we score four goals. That's how it is. What did I say, was the past like this? No, it's only what we have to do in this season, to create our own atmosphere for us and nobody else.'

This went to the very heart of Klopp's beliefs and his philosophy. He wanted to recreate a reasonable facsimile of Dortmund's Yellow Wall and where else to do so then a bouncing and heaving Anfield? That he was disappointed will be discussed, but initially the German was of the view that he had found a bastion of footballing romanticism: 'like no other club on earth, Anfield stands for this and now I'm here and am a truly happy man.'

Anfield, of course, can be an abnormally powerful stadium, a place of worship and one that can generate a match changing atmosphere. Anyone who doubts this need only glance at a YouTube video of Chelsea in 2005 or Manchester City (and that was an early kick-off) in 2014. However, during Klopp's tenure it became apparent to the German that there may have been a discord between his expectations and the actuality. Though capable of exhibiting hairs-on-back-of-neck moments as adulation, fervour and passion fill the air, so it can also be a cauldron of sibilant silence, of sighs of frustration and angst. A bemused Thomas Tuchel, speaking after his Dortmund side had been thrillingly beaten in that gooseflesh-inducing Europa League Quarter-Final had said, almost accusingly, that 'the stadium seemed to know what would happen. It was as if it was meant to be.' But Klopp would become intimately familiar with the fact that the more prosaic the encounter, the more exponentially negative effect on the crowd, unless of course, there were goals to cheer. Frequently in modern times (and, it has to be noted, undoubtedly throughout the decades), Anfield was a becalmed sea of muted red, of finger biting and nervous tension. Klopp wanted 'full-throttle football' and he felt he needed the storied 'twelfth man' to help him deliver on his vision. It has already become one of the enduring images of the German's reign as he, sometimes angrily, entreats the crowd to greater decibels of noise. Indeed, Klopp had been in borderline scolding form when, after Crystal Palace had inflicted a 2-1 victory (no, not that one - this one in late 2015) on the Reds at Anfield, he had declared:

'After the goal on eighty two minutes, with twelve minutes to go, I saw many people leave the stadium. I felt pretty alone at this moment. Of course, we decide when it's over. Between eighty two and ninety four, you can make eight goals if you want, you only have to work for it.'

Klopp had, and has, the standing and status to get away with a comment like this; imagine the furore had Rodgers or, heavens forbid, Hodgson uttered something similar. But he was right in that it was a calculated ploy to get the Anfield crowd fully behind the team, to make them feel truly at one with their side. In the home draw with West Bromwich Albion a few weeks later, the German again made a deliberate decision; this time on the other side of the emotional spectrum as he - to the mirthful delight of rival fans - gathered his team and saluted the Kop en masse. But the gleeful baying of bitter Bluenoses missed the point. This was merely Klopp seeking to compound the relationship between the Anfield faithful and his team. As he said himself:

'How could we say thank you to the fans? Send letters? You can only react at this moment, directly after the game. I didn't get the feeling that the Liverpool supporters in the stadium had a problem with what we did. In that situation, I would do it again.'

Klopp may have been giving the impression that this salute was impulsive but he was almost surely waiting for the perfect moment to seek to strike a chord of empathy and togetherness with the Liverpool supporters. As a humorous postscript, Jamie Redknapp - whose subtlety on a football pitch evidently never translated to a grasp of the concept in the pundit's chair - opined that '(A)s for Liverpool and Jurgen Klopp, I'm not sure about celebrating a 2-2 draw at home to West Brom in front of the Kop.' Some Liverpool fans also wailed as the pitchforks began to be metaphorically brandished on social media, but the reality is that Klopp was seeking to cajole the support. Nothing more, nothing less. It was a clever ploy in this hyper-competitive world the Reds now inhabit, as they seek to make the most of every tool at their disposal.

But, more than any other factor, Klopp will have to make his peace with the fact that there is an underlying current to the angst which can sometimes descend on Anfield. How he can solve this - short of more thrilling football like was witnessed in the autumn of 2016 - is, of course, another matter.

Because it is that elusive league title that Liverpool fans yearn for. It is largely this which gives rise to the sporadic instances of anxiety which can grip Anfield.

Allow me the indulgence of lapsing into an intermittent first person. I'm a fan of Liverpool Football Club and if you're reading this, you most probably are too. You're probably passionate, that zeal is probably all-encompassing. What drives that ardour if not a bittersweet longing for the Holy Grail? Perhaps that's stretching things a bit but Liverpool fans throughout the world are utterly and completely unique. A large part of this has to do with the character and special DNA of the club we support, some of it has to do with geography and politics, of scouse isolationism, exceptionalism and rebellion, of music and culture. But there is a portion that has to do with this long, dark night of the soul. This desert of hope and despair and the dance that plays out every year.

Neil Atkinson of *The Anfield Wrap* often exclaims that he wants to have a pint with Liverpool champions of England and I'm sure you can feel his longing. Most who are reading this - if you can remember the last league title at all that is - are peering back through a vortex of giddy highs and despairing lows to that almost eldritch era that was before the Premier League began. When the Cold War still lingered and threatened intermittently to heat up, when Thatcher and her cronies bestrode the British political landscape, when *Spitting Image* reigned supreme, when a shocking new epidemic took hold of portions of the country and conjured fear and loathing amongst a generation. The last time Liverpool won the title, *Home Alone* was a box office phenomenon and MC Hammer sang about not being able to touch this. And we can't touch it, the vast river of time is unceasing and flows on; the past becomes more and more intangible with every passing year. We feel like we can reach out and touch it but it is illusory, utterly ethereal and incorporeal.

This book may be chiefly concerned with Liverpool in the Premier League and I can appreciate that this very phrase will rankle with some Liverpool fans. Soz. All I can really remember is the Premier League but I still glory in our unique past. Because let's be very clear - and this is not any species of a scouse sense of misplaced entitlement, something we're mocked for incessantly the world over - Liverpool is part of a very select group of legendary football clubs in European football. Are Manchester City, for all their billions, or Chelsea members? Are PSG members? Are Atlético Madrid dining at this table? Are even Arsenal? Liverpool Football Club are royalty; historically and culturally we are genuine European aristocrats. Milan, Juventus, Barcelona, Real, Bayern and Manchester United are perhaps the only clubs that can rank alongside our dizzying and glorious achievements. Yes, the nature of our club, the fact that we may have sought for too long to hold onto the cultural heritage of Liverpool, the mythic and largely erroneous 'Liverpool way,' the conservative qualities that have been carefully cultivated over generations; all this and more (not least human disaster and tragedy) has led to rambling stagnation and frustration. But we retain the capacity for bouncing back, for recapturing glory. We're no Nottingham Forest or Aston Villa; Liverpool will never sink to that. We have painted our glory in large, bold strokes that are impossible to miss. And impossible to ignore. It's why we still inspire such hatred in rival clubs' fans, who may not want to admit it, but can always feel the breath that is Liverpool on their necks.

Emlyn Hughes once famously espoused that 'Liverpool are magic, Everton are tragic' and this adage still has more than a ring of truth to it. The Toffees cannot get over the halcyon days of their best side, when they briefly lit up the Football League. They blame the Reds, they wail through gnashed teeth that it was Liverpool's fault that they couldn't strut their stuff on the continent. They allowed themselves to plummet into a relative oblivion, a mire of mediocrity, energy sapping and source of crippling inertia. They went from Tony Cottee signing for a near British record to nearly getting relegated in the space of a few years. Our time in the comparative doldrums has sometimes been tough to live through, make no mistake, but we've won continental trophies, we've lit up Cardiff, we've been the highest ranked side in European competition.

We nearly won the league.

Yes, that phrase does indeed fester. Arguably, it should be outlawed in Liverpool lexicon. But there has to be an admission that the goalposts have shifted so considerably in the past twenty five years that Shankly's second is sometimes not so bad. We strive for first, of course we do, we thirst for it but in many ways it is a gnawing, grasping and insatiable agony that an alcoholic might recognise.

For years after just about getting their act together (on the field at least) in the Nineties, Liverpool sought to overthrow Manchester United and reclaim their league title. When the Reds finally managed to finish above their deadly rivals in 2002, Arséne Wenger's Arsenal put together a quite ridiculous run to claim the title; in 2009 Liverpool came up against possibly Ferguson's best ever United side. In the still raw wound that is 2014, the then most expensively assembled sporting team on the planet ensured that the woodwork again moved. Since the Premier League formed, our rivals have become legion and we have gone from a scenario in 1992 when we were close to United as favourites, onto the sugar daddy days of Blackburn Rovers, through to Wenger revolutionising the Gunners, to Chelsea and Manchester City producing lottery winning tickets. Now Spurs, once a veritable laughing stock, even in our darker days in the Premier League, have joined the party. We're looking at a big six that looks like it could be entrenched at the top of the league for years to come.

So can Liverpool win that league title?

Personally I believe that, under Klopp, we can. The achievements of 2016/17 have in some ways been underestimated because of the lopsided nature of the season. To paraphrase our German manager, we went from doubters to believers to doubters again. The run in was tough, the football uninspiring but it was a massively solid foundation upon which to build; Liverpool attained their goals. Flip the two halves of the season and all Liverpool fans are hugely positive with what we could be capable of going into the new season, not a million miles removed with how many felt in the autumn of 2013. Jamie Carragher, speaking in April of 2017, put it succinctly when he asserted that:

'I think Liverpool have got the sixth best squad in the league so to finish in the top four would be a very good season...you saw the reasons why they fell away in the middle of the season, they didn't have reinforcements, especially when Sadio Mane was gone to the African Cup of Nations. It's very difficult; they don't have the revenue to compete with the others, it will be a building process. It won't be a case of splashing the cash and going for the league next season. I think that it will be a gradual improvement, similar to when I was playing under Houllier and Benítez, when we built to a title challenge, we never quite pulled it off but we came very close on a number of occasions. If Liverpool can get into the top four for two or three years on the bounce, than that would be a major achievement. You cement your position in there and then maybe think, "Ok, let's go for the title"'.

In 2016, with the Reds struggling in the league but reigniting European dreams, Paul Tomkins wrote that (some) 'Liverpool fans wanted Klopp's Dortmund when he arrived but not the process that made Klopp's Dortmund so special: the time it took (over two years) and the development of young players from unheard-ofs into world class stars.' Some Kopites bemoan (what looks, at the time of writing) the imminent arrival of Álvaro Morata to United, forgetting that the Reds have never signed a bonafide world class star. Perhaps Torres or Suárez came closest but these had been looked at by other clubs and, for different reasons, there was hesitancy from the big-hitters. Moreover, it's not as if paying eye-watering sums of money is a guarantee for success; just look at Shevchenko, Ángel Di María, Verón or, em, Shaun Wright-Phillips.

But as these words are written in June after optimism had reigned for a few weeks following the confirmation of Champions League qualification only to be dashed upon another altar of bemusing decisions by FSG, there is always misgivings. The Virgil Van Dijk fiasco may have been resolved by the time you're reading this but the whole sorry story has again sullied the club. It could ultimately be proved to be media mongering or a show worthy of curtains and Christmas lights but the impression remains – and probably will for some time – that our owners sometimes leave the manager almost high and dry. There are echoes of the debacle over the tee-shirts in support of Suárez, when Kenny had to face the glare of the cameras in what felt like a vacuum of ill-support, in this latest mishandling of a situation. But then, it must be pointed out, mistakes happen. However, for Liverpool to truly compete and for the positive trajectory to be continued under Klopp, these errors have to be nullified. Ian Ayre has stepped down as CEO and has since gone on to an ill-fated term with 1860 Munich and his successor, Peter Moore, has an unenviably tough job on his hands. Moore, who has had stints with Reebok, Sega and Electronic Arts, may have lived in California but is a dyed in the red Liverpool fan and in 2009, when promoting *FIFA 10*, told *The Guardian* that:

'I've lived in America for 28 years now, but I'm a scouser by birth and football is my passion. My dad took me to Anfield when I was four, in 1959, and I've bled red ever since. I had the pleasure of getting involved with them when I was with Reebok, when we did the kit deal, which was a big thrill for me. But, yeah, I live and die Liverpool.'

Soon after taking on his new role, Moore was interviewed by *The Liverpool Echo* and, when asked about the challenges ahead, observed that:

' … I've sat down with my team and gone through a host of stuff, and I have been able to get a particular understanding of how the club is run from a financial basis. But I repeat, what we need to do is to continue to provide Jurgen and Michael with the resources, that's our remit, that's the key.'

The 'Michael' in question was, of course, Michael Edwards, Liverpool's new Sporting Director, who would reap a whirlwind of fan displeasure following the Van Dijk saga. At this stage, it is still hard to see what part – if any – Edwards (or, indeed, Moore) played in the furore that had supporters of the Reds everywhere going into a veritable meltdown. But it is probably the wisest course of action to hold off thorough judgment until September 1st, at the very earliest.

But Michael Edwards could possibly do himself a favour and cease to exist in a bubble of media silence, as this is no doubt irking many. The former Head of Performance and Analysis, who worked with both Kenny Dalglish and Brendan Rodgers, will, like his boss, have a tough time ahead convincing some sceptics. However, he brings many qualities to the role and has demonstrably proved capable in his many positions within the club. As Andy Kelly, writing in *The Echo*, put it:

'In June 2013 he was promoted to the role of director of technical performance and

was then made technical director in August of 2015, basically running football operations which had three main strands. First he instigated a fundamental change into the way Liverpool scout, both at first team and Academy levels, and oversees that. Second he continued to manage the analysis side of the club. The final string to his bow was setting up a research department at LFC, something which has since become commonplace at Premier League clubs.'

Whether Edwards can transfer his innovation in his plethora of roles thus far to a more specific one is, of course, the key question. Perhaps, though, it is for the best that he likes to keep a low profile as, short of signing Lionel Messi, Johan Cruyff and Billy Liddell, there will still be inevitable uproar from some sections of the fan base.

Finally, in regard to FSG, and to reiterate that there are reservations about their regime at the club, but an undoubted positive has been the potential £50 million transformation from the Kirkby Academy into a state-of-the-art training complex that would incorporate both the first team and the underage squads. Melwood being relatively far from the Academy (separated by five miles) had been a particular frustration of Klopp's since he came to the club and it is envisaged that the development of Kirkby – which will include the purchase of fourteen acres of land in Simonswood Playing Fields to expand the size of the complex to sixty acres – will allow those from the under-nines through to the first team to train together. Assuming planning permission is granted by Knowsley Metropolitan Borough Council, it is hoped that work will begin in early 2018, with Liverpool's first team squad commencing pre-season training at Kirkby in time for the 2019/20 campaign.

Why the hugely expensive and aspiring move? In July of 2016, Klopp gave his thoughts on the matter:

'We need to develop the club. We think about building a new Academy or bringing the Academy and Melwood together. Things like this – it's much longer term than my contract. It's important we do the right things so this wonderful club can be successful both in these six years but later on too. We are very responsible for the club.'

Responsible for the club. It could be argued that we can all own a part of that sentence. In even small ways, all that are reading these words can contribute to Liverpool Football Club. Not just supporting in the stadium; that's important, but there's so much more to it than that. I myself am not one of the privileged few that can make it to Anfield regularly; twice a season is my lot if I'm lucky. But, while we all get frustrated, while we can all howl in anxiety because we care so much, the fact remains that we all share in the mythology of this wonderful club. Don't accuse me of being overly romantic for claiming that support of Liverpool is a treasured birthright that can be passed from mother to son or from father to daughter. Because we are absolutely steeped in romanticism; the magic is palpable. That this sometimes, by some bleak alchemy, can change into a dark and forbidding enchantment is to be expected when passions run so high and deep. This football club does play with your soul, nibbles away at your innards, is the rat that Wilson shrank from in Orwell's room 101. But count yourself lucky that this is the case because the pay back for the periodical angst is a truly glorious one.

I can't tell the future, thankfully. I don't know if we'll ever get that league title that I crave for so much. I can't tell if I will ever be able to have that pint of ale, wallowing in the delicious truth that Liverpool are champions of England, glorying in the fact that we will be referred to as such for at least another eleven months. You may be reading this and seething at another botched transfer (which, of course, happens to every single professional club on the planet). Chelsea or Spurs may have beaten us to another promising Brazilian that few have us had heard of before the speculation began. Being the eighth richest club in the world is no good when we're only the fifth richest club in England, right? Well Tottenham are the sixth richest club in the Premier League and have been the best performing side over the past two years in England. Money will always be hugely important but the field is levelling to a degree. No more do minnows bow to their fate when confronted by circling sharks.

There is a paradox at the heart of Liverpool Football Club in the last twenty five years. The Reds are the most consistent English side of all time but only the fourth best since the formation of the Premier League. Liverpool is a club which has forged its worldwide reputation by showing sparkling and historic continental form but has only qualified for Europe's top competition on nine occasions since 1992 (but, Arsenal fans, we tend to make it count). The Reds suffered tragedy and heartache, human devastation on a near unimaginable level, at a time when football in England was just about to burst kaleidoscopically into the national collective consciousness. Ours has been an intoxicating brew of triumph and failure, of epic overachievement and sometimes baffling disappointment.

But through all those years that span the formation of the Premier League, this modern era that fluctuates and pulses with mystifying haste, there have been the moments that continue to define our club. There has been Souness as he surely speculated on his managerial future but witnessed five goals from a Toxteth teenager; Roy Evans – a genuine servant of the club – punching the air as Steve McManaman tied Bolton Wanderers in knots; the passing brilliance of Roy's side that came so close but just failed at final hurdles; Owen's speculative left footer that arrowed past a despairing and disbelieving David Seaman in the Cardiff summer sun; Gerrard firing past Barthez to incredulous celebration across the globe; Gary Mac's injury time winner in Dortmund; Gary Mac's injury time winner in Liverpool; Danny Murphy's lob to wipe the smug smile from Ferguson's face for the fourth time in a row; Stevie's screamer prompting ecstatic exclaim from a bluenose; García's dipping, improbable effort past the best goalkeeper in the world that made us first believe; the Anfield crowd against Chelsea; the crowd at half time in the Atatürk; Carragher's refusal to lie down and subsequent leap for joy; Stevie's forty yard bullet in a final that will forever be remembered in his honour; Kuyt's penalty in the Champions' League Semi-Final to vanquish the Blues again; Fernando Torres; 4-1 in Old Trafford; Madrid hit for four;

Kenny's return before an ocean of red adoration and Kenny's tears when he secured a trophy; Suárez tormenting canaries on multiple occasions; Suarez tormenting the league; Brendan Rodgers' face as 'You'll Never Walk Alone' belted out of the Anfield speakers prior to beating City 3-2 on the twenty fifth anniversary of Hillsborough; Klopp laughing and cajoling and remonstrating; Lovren's header in the dying minutes against Dortmund; Sturridge's glorious opener against Sevilla that should never be forgotten; Mané torturing a traumatised Gunners' rearguard to make it 4-1; those gorgeous Reds in the months that followed as we again whispered about league titles.

There are so many more and sincerest apologies if your favourite one has been forgotten. Indeed, if I was to write these words again tomorrow the list would probably look very different. So glory in that, wallow in it and taste it. Don't dwell on the heartache or allow frustration to get the better of you.

We may be still waiting on that Premier League title, but, in reality, it's been anything but a barren desert.

ADDITIONAL THANKS TO TTT BENEFACTORS:

Ahmed El Maghraby
Aiden Halloran
Alan Lamb
Alan Raleigh
Alkesh Dudhaiya
Allan Høy-Simonsen
Allen Baynes
Andrew Argyle
Andrew Chow
Andy Coles
Anthony Rodenhurst
Anton Black
Axel Loecken
Banerjee Saugato
Ben Atherton
Bernard Wright
Bernd Schorr
Bernt Milne Grieg
Bijin Benesh
Brian Davis
Charles Morrish
Chris Bracebridge
Chris Tang
Christine Andrade
Christoph Tung
Christopher Bruno
Christopher Sewards
Colin Whiting
David Evans
David O'Reilly
David Perkins
Deena Naidoo
Dominic Thomas
Donald Rock
Eamonn Turbitt
Edward Alkins
Edward Robinson

Francis Tan
Gareth McMahon
Gary Fowler
George Ebbs
Gina Hoagland
Glenn Perris
Glenn Ticehurst
Gøran Schytte
Greg Vinikoor
Gudmund Krogsrud
Guy Parr
Haluk Arpacioglu
Iain Bundred
Ilan Shaw
Iyad Zahlan
Jan Ove Knudseth
Jason Charles Rowe
Jassim Jamal
Jesper Marcussen
Joe Power
John Clarke
John Goldie
John Gordon
John Nolan
John Penton
Jonas Luul
Jonathan Sowler
Kostadin Galabov
Mohammad Al Sager
Mohsin Meghji
Neil Gold
Niall O'Harte
Nick Hall
Nick Mundon
Omar Arnason
Patricia Jill
Adamiecki

Patrick Smith
Paul Mays
Paul McCormack
Paul Morgan
Peder Markus Topp
Peter Barber
Peter Cooke
Peter Doyle
Peter J Robinson
Peter Verinder
Phillip Collins
Quinn Emmett
Robert Moore
Robert Sangster
Rolv Hoel
Rupert Eve
Ryonadai
Sacha Pettitt
S. Periathiruvadi
Sergio Trevino
Simon Ashton
Simon Barrington
Stephen Capel
Stephen Farr-Jones
Stephen Rowland
Steve Lucy
Steve McCarthy
Stuart Lloyd
Stratoe Koutsouridis
Suzanne Wiseman
Thomas McCool
Tony Stringer
Tristan Wyse
Vidar Kjøpstad
Waqas Kaiser
Western Ivey
Yau Choi Yeung

Printed in Great Britain
by Amazon